The World by Sea

100 Legendary Cruise Destinations

ROUGH GUIDES

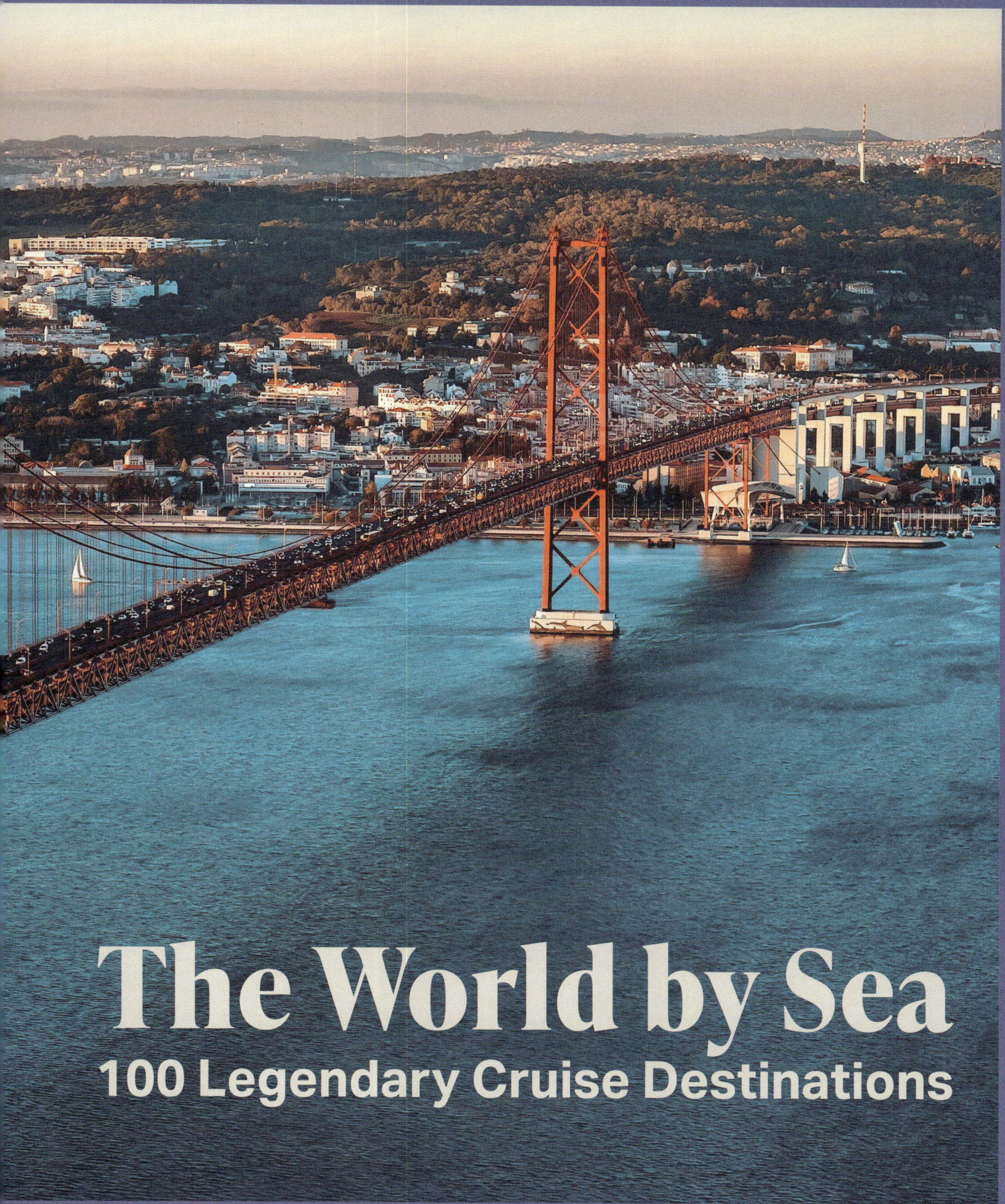

The World by Sea

100 Legendary Cruise Destinations

The World by Sea

100 Legendary Cruise Destinations

Introduction

For many travellers the romance of cruising begins with a skyline rising from the sea – domes, towers, cliffs, or a line of palms – and the enticing promise that tomorrow's horizon will look nothing like today's.

This book gathers 100 ports and cruising destinations that are truly legendary, from world-famous capitals where history is written in stone to small harbours whose names still feel like a secret. You'll step ashore in cities that glitter with modern ambition, then trade streets for wilderness where ice, desert or rainforest presses right to the water's edge. Islands come shaped in every form, presenting volcanic crescents, coral rings, wind-scoured outposts and lush hideaways scented with spice. Along the way are places shaped by empires, pilgrimages and trade winds, and others heady with music, food and street life.

The selected ports of call mix marquee stops with offbeat detours to keep curiosity at the helm. From midnight sun to warm seas and the thrill of landfall, these 100 destinations are an invitation to start plotting routes long before the journey has even begun.

Note: Where primary cruising destinations are accessed by a port with a different name, the latter is given in brackets in the place title.

Western Mediterranean

The western Mediterranean offers cruising at its most seductive, presenting a sweep of sun-warmed stone, glittering harbours, citrus-scented hillsides and coastlines shaped by empire, art and appetite. Here, Gothic spires, Roman ruins, myriad cliff-hung villages, characterful old ports and volcanic shores rise from a sea of blue and gold. It is a region of colour, contrast and irresistible pleasures, made for long looks and lingering arrivals.

Barcelona

SPAIN

Barcelona is the Mediterranean's great show-off, and the swagger starts right by the water, with its sparkling harbour, a promenade that runs past Barceloneta, and a long sweep of city beaches that makes the place feel like the world's most cultural holiday resort. Inland, the medieval old town tightens into a labyrinth of Gothic lanes and hidden squares, before the city snaps open into the Eixample's grid, where modernista façades ripple and twist with unmistakable confidence. Gaudí's great, still not-quite-finished Sagrada Família sums up the mood – ambitious, restless, impossible to ignore – but the city's energy is just as present in its markets, thriving music scene and late-lunch, bar-hopping tapas culture. It can be crowded, especially in peak season, yet step beyond the obvious corridors and Barcelona still surprises with its neighbourhood grit, design flair and a proud Catalan identity.

(L) Amidst the chimneys on the rooftop of Gaudí's Casa Milà

Rome (Civitavecchia)

ITALY

Rome is a city that rewards drifting. You can plan the classics, but some of the best moments arrive unannounced: stumbling on the Trevi Fountain in the early light, ducking into the Pantheon and looking up into the widest dome in the world, or crossing a piazza that suddenly feels like the centre of everything. Layers stack up everywhere – ancient temples beneath churches, Baroque fountains in front of palazzi – yet the place never feels like a museum piece. The big-hitters are non-negotiable, from the Roman Forum and Palatine's evocative sprawl to the Vatican Museums' overwhelming riches, but Rome's real seduction lies in how casually it delivers grandeur alongside daily life. Finish like a local, with gelato and a slow wander through the early evening buzz.

(O) The Roman Forum; (L) Monumento Nazionale a Vittorio Emanuele II; (T) Alfresco dining; (B) The mighty Colosseum

Amalfi Coast (Salerno/Sorrento) *ITALY*

The Amalfi Coast is one of Europe's most dramatic stretches of shoreline: cliffs dropping almost sheer into the sea, a corniche road curling above the water, and villages engineered against common sense, their houses clinging limpet-like to rock. From the water, the whole coast looks even more improbable, with its flowered terraces, Saracen towers on outcrops, and green peninsulas stretching into the haze. On land, the pleasures are as much vertical as horizontal, thanks to hidden stairways, lemon-scented lanes and head-spinning footpaths like the Sentiero degli Dei. Positano may hog the limelight, but Amalfi still hints at a life beyond tourism, and tiny Atrani is an often-overlooked gem. It's busy, and no denying that it's expensive, but few places feel so instantly cinematic.

(O) Positano from the sea; (L) Quintessential Amalfi Coast features; (T) Ceramic platters for sale in Positano

Marseille *FRANCE*

(T) Yachts in port in Marseille

Marseille has always been a port city first and foremost, making it an unmissable Mediterranean cruise stop. The Vieux Port is the natural starting point, an intoxicating mix of water, sunlight and constant activity framed by twin forts and lined with cafés and seafood restaurants. Look past the grit and you'll find a metropolis with real magnetism, that is culturally cosmopolitan, garrulous and stubbornly down-to-earth. Recent years have brought a new waterfront focus and headline architecture, yet Marseille still surprises with corners that feel like fishing villages hiding inside a big industrial city. Beyond town, the coastline turns wild and white, with the Calanques National Park offering fjord-like inlets and crystal-clear water, carefully managed to protect the fragile landscape.

Sicily (Taormina/Catania)

ITALY

Eastern Sicily packs dramatic contrasts into a compact, compelling sweep. Taormina sits on a crag above the Ionian, festooned with bougainvillea and backed by mountains, its ancient Greek theatre set up for maximum drama and still used for summer performances. It has long drawn writers and bohemians and, for all the crowds, the setting remains irresistibly (and fittingly) theatrical. Catania is the tougher, more contemporary counterpoint: a vibrant historic centre built after the 1693 earthquake in black lava and creamy limestone, enlivened by a raucous fish market, student energy and a proper nightlife scene. Then there's Etna, looming above it all, Europe's highest volcano and still highly active, shaping towns, roads and the very stone of the buildings. Few places distil Sicily's beauty and edge so vividly as the combination of these destinations.

(O) The ruins of Taormina's theatre; (L) Sicilian "teste di moro", a typical souvenir; (T) Dinner under colourful umbrellas in Catania; (B) Piazza Bellini in Catania

SERVIZIO
GONDOLE

Adriatic & Ionian Mediterranean

The Adriatic and Ionian seas showcase the Mediterranean at its most luminous and layered, offering a world of pale stone, terracotta roofs, pine-dark islands and mountain-backed bays. Here, empires have left their marks in marble streets, sea walls, campaniles and old harbours, while the water shifts from silver to sapphire beneath steep limestone coasts. Arriving by sea presents glorious views that embody both crumbling open-air history and sunshine escapes.

Venice *ITALY*

(T) Gondolas on Venice's Grand Canal

Venice arrives with a sense of déjà vu – the palaces on the Canal Grande, Piazza San Marco's film-set perfection – then quickly becomes strange again once you notice the everyday logistics: furniture being winched from barges, fishermen knee-deep in lagoon water, life adapted to a city built on mudflats. Founded on a cluster of islands, Venice grew dense and intricate, tied together by hundreds of bridges and divided into *sestieri* that each reward aimless wandering. The showpiece monuments are as lavish as promised, from San Marco's mosaic-clad splendour to the Palazzo Ducale's Gothic swagger, yet the city's appeal is in the accumulation of details, from a quiet *campo* to an atmospheric wine bar or the buzz of Rialto market, where locals still outnumber tourists. There's no denying that visiting Venice by cruise ship is contentious due to the environmental impact; consider routes that dock in Trieste or Ravenna instead.

Dubrovnik *CROATIA*

Dubrovnik's historic core feels suspended in time: a medieval maritime city reshaped after the 1667 earthquake, with churches and palaces blending seamlessly with green-shuttered stone houses inside formidable walls. Its long history as Ragusa, a fiercely independent trading republic, still seems written into the limestone streets, sea gates and defensive towers. The setting is half the story, too – a sea-battered town under a grizzled mountain, with ramparts rising proudly over the Adriatic. Walking the walls is the essential first task, giving a perfect vantage over tiled roofs, bell towers and sparkling water. Dubrovnik's modern screen fame has led to a surge in day-trippers, and the old town can tip into theme-park mode at midday, but the city's deeper pull remains intact – its tradition of independence, scars and recovery from the 1990s siege, and a coastline that begs lingering, whether on the wooded island of Lokrum or up on Mount Srđ for panoramic views.

(L) Dubrovnik's city walls and harbour; (T) The city from a nearby hillside; (B) Istrian grilled fish for dinner

Split

CROATIA

With its seafront cafés and ancient alleyways, shouting stallholders and travellers in transit, bustling, exuberant Split is one of the Mediterranean's most compelling cities. It has a unique historical heritage too, having grown out of the palace built here by the Roman Emperor Diocletian in AD 295. Diocletian's Palace remains the city's central ingredient, having been gradually transformed into a warren of houses, tenements, churches and chapels by the various peoples who came to live here after his successors had departed. The city is famous for the vivacious outdoor life that takes over the streets in all but the coldest and wettest weather: as long as the sun is shining, the swish cafés of the waterfront Riva are never short of custom. Split is also a hub, with potential for easy side trips to Roman Salona or nearby fortresses, as well as ferries that connect the nearby islands of Brač and Hvar.

(O) A view of Diocletian's Palace; (L) Inside the palace's walls; (T) The ancient Roman town of Salona; (B) Stone lions guard the entrance to the Cathedral of St Domnius within Diocletian's Palace

Kotor *MONTENEGRO*

Kotor's approach is a slow reveal through the Bay of Kotor, a steep-sided inlet ringed by towering mountains that makes the Adriatic feel suddenly Alpine. The walled, medieval city sits at the south-east corner of the Bay of Kotor, an irregularly shaped triangle of terracotta-tiled rooftops, bordered by the steep, craggy foothills of Lovćen, the River Škurda and the sea. First colonized by the Greeks, passed through Serb, Austro-Hungarian and Bosnian hands before fifteenth-century Ottoman conquests forced it under the protective wing of Venice until 1797. The resulting old town is compact and beautifully preserved, enclosing cafés and churches galore. The old fortress walls sit proudly above the town, and make for a rewarding climb to St Ivan's Castle, best begun from the North Gate; the castle gives tremendous views of the fjord. Though no longer Europe's best-kept secret, Kotor's elevation has failed to dim the timeless delights of its cobbled alleyways and secluded piazzas.

(L) Colourful shutters on a Kotor shop; (T) Kotor lit up at twilight; (B) A guard in traditional Montenegrin folk costume

Corfu

GREECE

The island of Corfu has a lushness that much of Greece only hints at, with deep green hills set against a mountainous skyline, and water that shifts from turquoise to midnight blue as the coast bends. Beaches are part of the island's appeal, from soft sand to pebble coves backed by dramatic scenery, but its real charm lies in Corfu Old Town, or Kérkyra, where Venetian influence lingers in arcaded streets, shaded squares and elegant courtyards. The Liston promenade, modelled on Paris's Rue de Rivoli, sets the tone for café life and people-watching, while the island's layered past adds a lightly-worn texture. Corfu can be sampled quickly – a swim and a wander – but it rewards a slower rhythm. Dip into a backstreet taverna, stroll down the back streets and prepare to marvel at a viewpoint opening suddenly onto the Ionian. Easy-going yet quietly distinctive, it offers beauty with depth and charm.

(O) The old town's colourful rooftops; (L) A narrow street in Corfu Old Town; (T) Paleokastritsa on Corfu

Aegean & Eastern Mediterranean

The Aegean and Eastern Mediterranean are bright, ancient and charged with movement: a world of whitewashed islands, honeyed stone, blue-domed horizons and harbours crafted by trade, empire and myth. Here, classical ruins, volcanic cliffs, fortified cities and spice-scented waterways rise from seas of startling colour. Dazzling contrasts and deep histories pervade every corner, where each new shore carries the promise of discovery.

Athens (Piraeus) GREECE

Athens is the rare capital where an ancient rock still dominates daily life. The Acropolis crowns almost every view, and the Parthenon's presence is as symbolic as it is physical, yet modern Athens is no sepia postcard. It's loud, late and lived outdoors, where cafés stay packed into the small hours and neighbourhoods reward anyone who strays beyond the obvious circuit. First impressions can be frazzled – postwar growth wasn't kind – but investment and pedestrianization have helped the centre breathe again, and the city's famously intimate "largest village" feel comes through quickly. The essentials remain unmissable, from the Acropolis itself to the National Archaeological Museum's unrivalled collection, then the rest of the day can be as simple as market streets, watching views of the Parthenon change with the light, and lingering outdoor meals. The major cruise and ferry port of Piraeus makes it all wonderfully easy to reach.

(L) The Caryatid Porch of the Erechtheion on the Acropolis, a masterpiece of ancient Greek architecture

Santorini

GREECE

Santorini's appeal begins with a geological shock. The caldera is the scar of a colossal volcanic explosion: a crater-rim of cliffs that turns the island into an amphitheatre of light and sea. The raw spectacle is undeniable – white villages perched on the rim, a sheer drop to the water, and the strange thrill of standing on the edge of a volcano's aftermath. It is this drama that makes Santorini one of the great icons of the Cyclades, instantly recognizable, deeply photogenic and still able to deliver an impact when the light begins to soften and the whole caldera shifts colour. Beyond the famous viewpoints, quieter corners reveal a more spacious beauty taking in black-sand beaches, volcanic slopes, blue-domed chapels and paths that open suddenly onto the vast bowl of the caldera. Look back across that flooded crater and the island's strange, cinematic scale does the rest.

(O) The iconic domed rooftops of Oia, Santorini; (L) Greek salad and seafood; (T) The black sand beach of Perissa

Mykonos *GREECE*

Mykonos is the Cyclades at full volume: a teeming main town, famous beaches and a nightlife scene that can run until dawn. Yet behind the glamour there's a reason it was the first of the islands to be "discovered" by foreign visitors. Mykonos Town is a whitewashed maze of lanes designed to disorient, now crammed with restaurants, boutiques and bars, with the famous windmills providing the classic silhouette. It's easy to dismiss the island as a party stop, but even a short visit can be pure pleasure if you lean into its strengths – wander as early as you can, while the streets are still calm, save the heat for the beach, then come back as the crowds thicken and the town becomes its own kind of theatre. On a cruise itinerary, Mykonos is a classic stop because it offers instant, high-impact atmosphere, with that particular Aegean mix of beauty and buzz.

(L) Watching the waves on Mykonos Town's beach; (T) The island's famed white windmills; (B) Colourful fishing boats

Valletta *MALTA*

Valletta punches far above its weight. Malta's Baroque capital is compact enough to absorb on foot, yet dense with major museums, lavish churches and handsome fortifications that turn sea views into part of the architecture. If you only visit one place in Malta, it should be this, not least for the way the city balances grandeur with a modern edge. Leafy gardens, hip bars and restaurants abound, tucked into streets where honey-coloured stone catches the light and throws it back at the harbours on either side. The setting matters too, with remnants of Malta's distinctive culture sitting alongside the practical logic of a city built to defend an island at the cross-roads of empires. For cruisers, Valletta is a gift: the sights are close, the atmosphere is immediate, and a few hours can still feel like a proper encounter rather than a rushed dash.

(L) The courtyard garden at Casa Rocca Piccola

Istanbul *TÜRKIYE*

Istanbul is a city that refuses to fit in one frame. It stands astride Europe and Asia, split by the Bosphorus, and carries the weight of being capital to consecutive Christian and Islamic empires, a history written into its domes, minarets and formidable walls. The essential sights are astonishing, from the Hagia Sophia's monumental space to Topkapı's palaces and gardens, and the Grand Bazaar's restless commerce. Yet Istanbul is also Türkiye's economic and cultural engine, a go-ahead modern city where İstiklal Caddesi surges with nightlife energy and ferries stitch neighbourhoods into a vibrant tapestry. The Bosphorus itself is the perfect lens, floating past villas, fortresses and bridges before you plunge back into the streets. Seen from its waters, Istanbul's power comes into focus, with its heady mix of empire, trade, faith and modern life.

(L) The Hagia Sophia from the water; (T) The Imperial Hall in Topkapı Palace; (B) Traditional Turkish coffee

Northern Europe

Europe's northernmost reaches offer sea-fringed landscapes at their most elemental: fjords cut deep into mountain shadow, waterfalls dropping from impossible heights, Arctic horizons glowing under midnight sun, and volcanic landscapes steaming at the edge of the Atlantic. Between wild coasts and elegant northern capitals, the mood shifts from raw grandeur to quiet sophistication. This is a region of clean light, deep water and thrilling, far-flung approaches.

Geirangerfjord *NORWAY*

(T) Dramaric Geirangerfjord in summer

With its narrow, sheer, rugged walls and big-splash waterfalls, Geirangerfjord is Fjord Norway distilled to a single, dramatic cut in the landscape. It's one of the smallest major fjords, a convoluted offshoot of the Storfjord, yet it somehow feels outsized, in the way that the cliffs press in, the water turns a deep, glinting blue-black, and every bend reveals another vertiginous angle. A village anchors either end of the snake-like profile – Geiranger with the smarter hotels and crowds, Hellesylt quieter and closer to onward wild country – but the real point is being out on the water, letting the scale do the talking. Above the waterline, abandoned farms still cling improbably to ledges, a reminder that this overwhelming scenery was once a hard-won working landscape.

Flåm (Sognefjord)

NORWAY

Flåm's setting is the hook, with meadows and orchards at the water's edge, the Aurlandsfjord stretching away like a slender, secretive branch of the Sognefjord, and mountains rising so steeply they seem to press against the village. Around the station and quay the mood can be busy, but the bustle is easily forgiven when the scenery is this immediate. The Flåm Railway is the classic excursion, climbing from fjord level towards Myrdal through tunnels, ravines and waterfall country in one of Norway's great feats of mountain engineering. The water offers an equally strong claim, especially the route into nearby Nærøyfjord, where sheer cliffs, dark reflections and lonely farms turn the landscape almost severe. Flåm is an ideal entry point into the local landscapes because everything feels close at hand: railway, fjord, valley and mountain, all compressed into one compact, spectacular pocket of western Norway.

(L) The church and graveyard in Flåm

Bergen *NORWAY*

Bergen earns its "Gateway to the Fjords" tag by being far more than a staging post. Disembark into a city that still wears its maritime past on its sleeve, with old trading houses lining the Bryggen harbour district like a lived-in museum set. Torget's fish market keeps things satisfyingly salty, and the centre's tight lanes quickly pull you into everyday Bergen. It's a place of culture as much as scenery, from the big-ticket performing arts of early summer festival season to the contemporary pulse at USF Verftet, an old sardine factory repurposed into the city's standout arts complex. Come for the fjords, by all means, but linger for the mix of history, sea air and a nightlife that feels genuinely local rather than visitor-engineered.

(L) Bergen's historic centre; (T) Bryggen, a UNESCO World Heritage Site; (B) A prawn-mayonnaise open sandwich

Longyearbyen

SVALBARD, NORWAY

Longyearbyen feels like the last proper town before the map melts into ice, fjord and weather. In summer there's continuous daylight and a surprising softness to the tundra, with wild flowers and a busy cast of Arctic wildlife offshore and on land; in winter, the polar night takes over and the cold becomes a fact rather than a forecast. The settlement's story is entangled with coal, sovereignty and survival, yet it's increasingly defined by research and by travellers chasing the remote and the extreme. Between excursions, the excellent Svalbard Museum gives the place context – history, environment, and the practical realities of living this far north. Even a simple stroll near the water's edge comes with that bracing sense of scale: mountains, fjord, and a silence that makes most other "wilderness" destinations feel tame.

(O) Bright cabins at the foot of mountains in Longyearbyen; (L) Wild reindeer in Svalbard in summer; (T) The Northern Lights, visible over Svalbard; (B) Venturing onto the Arctic ice

Reykjavík

ICELAND

Reykjavík is compact and cosmopolitan, its narrow streets lined with small, brightly painted buildings that pop under wild Arctic light, with the steely North Atlantic surging into bays and inlets right at the edge of town. The skyline has its own quiet drama, from the basalt-inspired tower of Hallgrímskirkja to the glassy, light-catching Harpa concert hall on the waterfront, signalling a confident, can-do ambition, but the city's real genius is how it makes the elements liveable. Geothermal water warms buildings and even keeps winter streets from icing, while the public pools double as social clubs. Take a harbour stroll to soak up public art and sculptures, sea views, and the sense that whales and seabirds are never far away. It's a rare capital that feels instantly navigable yet still plugged into Iceland's bigger drama, with glaciers, volcanoes, lava fields and day-trip wildness hovering just beyond the city limits.

(O) Leif Erikson Memorial at the Hallgrímskirkja; (L) View from the Harpa concert hall; (T) Watching the sunset by the "Sun Voyager" sculpture

Akureyri *ICELAND*

Akureyri sits at the hinge-point of northeast Iceland. While it is an accessible town, its location is remote enough that the landscape still runs the show. From here, the region opens into a thinly populated expanse where the headline acts are volcanic – Mývatn's hot springs and formations, still visibly active in places – and elemental, from glacial rivers shouldering through gorges to summer whale-watching out of nearby Húsavík. It's the kind of port where a single day ashore can turn into a choose-your-own-adventure: soak in a geothermal spa with lake views, chase the roar of Dettifoss, or take the slower option and drive into open country that barely seems inhabited. Akureyri's appeal is that it puts Iceland's raw north within easy reach without sacrificing comfort.

(L) Dettifoss's majestic falls; (T) The town centre; (B) Relaxing in a geothermal forest lagoon

STORE CLAUS

Copenhagen

DENMARK

Copenhagen has spent the last decade collecting superlatives – for quality of life, cycling, design and food – yet it still feels relaxed and oddly homely once you're on the ground. Part of the charm is its hybrid personality, comprised of a Scandinavian capital with a gaze that also takes in London, Berlin and Amsterdam – which shows in everything from its architecture to its ease with reinvention. The city's "cool" is rarely performative; it's woven into daily routines, whether that's (literally) pedalling between neighbourhoods or drifting from waterfront to museum without much effort. Copenhagen rewards curiosity quickly and generously, in its acess to culture without strain, its wealth of food with real ambition, and its waterside ease that gives the whole city its quietly confident charm.

(L) Copenhagen from its harbour

Stockholm

SWEDEN

Stockholm's seduction is spatial, forged by water everywhere, light shifting across the city, and neighbourhoods that feel distinct even when they are only a bridge, ferry or cobbled lane apart. This is a capital shaped by its maritime setting, with the archipelago as both backdrop and playground, and with water acting less like an edge than a thread running through daily life. Gamla Stan draws visitors in first, all narrow streets, ochre façades and historic heft, with Stockholm Palace and Storkyrkan anchoring the old core. Beyond it, Stockholm's real strength is how effortlessly it moves between past and present – the Vasa Museum's astonishing salvaged warship, Djurgården's leafy museums and waterside walks, grand institutions, everyday cafés, polished design and lived-in corners. It is a city best experienced in layers: an elegant harbour-side first impression, an intimate wander through the historic centre, then a boat ride or island stroll that confirms the water is actually the main street here.

(O) Relaxing on the pier at Munkbrohamnen in Gamla Stan; (L) View from Stockholm City Hall towards Gamla Stan; (T) A guard in traditional blue uniform outside Stockholm Palace; (B) Cycling by the water

British Isles

The United Kingdom and Republic of Ireland offer a seafaring world of prominent weather and deep green drama. Here you will see castle-topped skylines, whisky-coloured hills, cliff paths, Georgian streets and harbours shaped by migration, trade and myth. On these isles, grandeur sits close to wildness, and lively capitals give way quickly to Highland glens, islands and Atlantic edges. The mood is storied and atmospheric, with history never far from the shore.

Edinburgh (South Queensferry) *SCOTLAND*

Sailing into the Firth of Forth with Edinburgh on the skyline feels like arriving through a history book, except the pages are alive with sea wind and gulls. South Queensferry's great show is the trio of bridges spanning the estuary, a layered statement of engineering that frames the approach beautifully. From the port it's a quick leap into Edinburgh itself, where the city's drama comes from its split personality: medieval closes and volcanic crags rubbing shoulders with Georgian order and wide civic spaces. The Scottish capital offers a great density of reward – castles, views, museums, pubs within close proximity – without sprawl. Even if you do nothing more than climb to Arthur's Seat for a vantage point and let the view do its work, Edinburgh still feels like a "best of" in one sweep.

(O) Edinburgh's historic skyline; (L) Atop Arthur's Seat; (T) Colourful shops line Victoria Street

Scottish Highlands (Invergordon) *SCOTLAND*

Invergordon is the threshold to the eastern Highlands. The Cromarty Firth has a workmanlike edge, with oil rigs and service vessels against the water, but beyond it the landscape quickly opens into broader Scottish drama: green slopes, sudden lochs, castle roads, whisky valleys and big, brooding skies. This is Highland country in concentrated form, rich in atmosphere as much as scenery. Cawdor Castle brings gardens, turrets and Shakespearean associations; Culloden carries the weight of clan history in its open, wind-scoured battlefield; and Loch Ness adds the long, dark sweep of one of Scotland's most mythologised landscapes, with Urquhart Castle broken beautifully on its shore. Distilleries deepen the sense of place, grounding the romance in barley, copper, oak and time. Within a few miles, the Cromarty Firth gives way to the Scotland visitors hope for: castles with stories attached, distilleries breathing malt into the air, and lochs dark enough to hold their myths.

(O) Invergordon is a deep water port visited by cruise ships for tours in the Highlands; (L) Urquhart Castle; (T) Culloden battlefield; (B) Traditional bagpipers

pier hotel
SEA TOURS
FRESH FISH
BRD 18

Isle of Skye (Portree)

SCOTLAND

The Isle of Skye announces itself in dramatic scenery and weather, with Portree serving as its compact, colourful gateway. The harbour is memorable enough in its own right – a small bowl of water, boats rocking at their moorings, bright houses along the quay and hills rising behind – but the island's real drama begins almost immediately beyond town. To the north, the Trotternish Peninsula gathers Skye's most theatrical landscapes into a single sweep: the Old Man of Storr standing in jagged silhouette, the Quiraing buckling into landslips and pinnacles, Kilt Rock dropping sharply to the sea, and the Fairy Glen folding green cones and miniature hills into something stranger than prettiness. Even a short journey inland brings that unmistakable Skye sensation of the road entering older, rougher country. Skye's reward is how quickly the landmarks stack up within sight of Portree's harbour.

(O) Portree Harbour's colourful houses line the shore;
(L) Fairy Glen hills; (T) Bobbing boats in the harbour at sunset

Belfast

NORTHERN IRELAND

Belfast has the energy of a city that's decided it won't be defined by old narratives. The waterfront is the obvious starting point, especially where shipbuilding history has been reclaimed as a modern visitor draw – not least the impressive Titanic Belfast museum – but the real pleasure is how quickly you can move from big, outward-facing statements to neighbourhood texture. There's a grit and humour to Belfast that plays well with its revived confidence: a place for galleries, live music and pubs that still feel rooted in the everyday. For cruise travellers, it's also a gateway to landscapes that feel dramatically close – the Antrim coast, causeways, glens – yet Belfast itself rewards time, especially if you like cities that are candid rather than polished. It's a city with undeniable edge, but also great warmth.

(L) Belfast City Hall

Dublin *IRELAND*

(T) The iconic Temple Bar

Dublin's appeal is immediate: a capital with literary heft, Georgian grace and enough talk, wit and momentum to keep the day moving even when it was meant to slow down. The River Liffey gives the city its spine, while Trinity College, the Book of Kells, Dublin Castle and the great sweep of Merrion Square and St Stephen's Green set out its historic and cultural range. Yet Dublin's real pull lies in the ease with which formality gives way to life on the street. A morning of museums, libraries and dignified façades can slide naturally into a bookshop browse, a pub session, or a conversation that becomes a miniature lecture on poetry, politics or where to find the best pint. Compact, expressive and endlessly human, Dublin is a city built as much on voice and vibes as on stone.

Cork (Cobh) *IRELAND*

Cork is an Irish urban highlight, with Cobh providing one of the most atmospheric approaches in the country. Cobh's harbour rises in a steep, colourful sweep above the water, crowned by the neo-Gothic bulk of St Colman's Cathedral, and its history adds immediate weight: this was the *Titanic*'s final port of call in 1912, and for generations one of Ireland's great departure points for emigrants crossing the Atlantic. From there, the focus shifts inland to Cork itself, a city with a quick tongue, a strong appetite and a fierce sense of its own identity. The River Lee splits around the centre, giving the streets an island-like shape, while the English Market supplies the essential introduction: fish stalls, farmhouse cheeses, spiced beef, cafés and the everyday theatre of Cork food culture under one roof. Around it are riverside quays, pubs with live music, independent shops, Georgian fragments and local-feeling neighbourhoods. Within easy reach, Blarney Castle adds the famous stone and wooded grounds, while Kinsale brings colour, seafood and Atlantic air.

(L) Tidy houses and St Colman's Cathedral in Cobh; (T) Pub life in Cork; (B) Old Head of Kinsale, Co Cork

European Atlantic Coast

The European Atlantic Coast feels open, weather-worn and restlessly maritime: a region of river mouths, island gardens, volcanic outposts, surf-edged headlands and cities developed by trade, migration and reinvention. Here, tiled hillsides, green mountains, pilgrimage routes, avant-garde museums and canal-threaded streets all face the same vast ocean. It is a coast of departures and arrivals, where salt air gives every place a sense of movement.

Lisbon *PORTUGAL*

(T) Santuário de Cristo Rei surveys the Tagus river and Lisbon's waterfront

Lisbon is vibrant, sunlit and unmistakably cool, a city of steep hills, river light, tiled façades and neighbourhoods that still feel lived-in rather than staged. The Tagus gives it breadth and brightness, but the city's real character is forged by its hilly topography: the climb through Alfama's lanes, Bairro Alto's evening hum, Chiado's elegant streets and viewpoints where red roofs tumble towards the water. It is a capital with confidence and texture: historic trams rattling past street art, grand squares opening onto café terraces, *azulejo*-covered walls catching the sun, and a food scene that runs from old-school seafood counters to inventive modern kitchens. Belém adds monumentality and maritime memory, while MAAT and LX Factory showcase the city's appetite for reinvention. Lisbon's appeal lies in its balance of being nostalgic but forward-looking, relaxed but alive, beautiful without ever feeling too polished.

Madeira (Funchal)

PORTUGAL

Funchal comes with pedigree: Madeira has been drawing travellers for centuries with its mild climate, clear Atlantic water, botanical richness and old-world glamour. The city sits in a natural amphitheatre, backed by steep green hills that make everything feel vertical and vivid, from the harbourfront and painted old-town doors to terraces heavy with flowers, fruit and sea views. It's accessible, but with real visual drama. In town, there are gardens, markets, museums, cafés and Madeira wine lodges to explore; beyond it, the island rises quickly into a wilder world of *levada* walks, laurel forest, highland trails and cloud-brushed peaks. Madeira's engineering is part of the spectacle too, with roads and tunnels cut through mountains and villages clinging to improbable slopes. Funchal feels instantly holiday-like, but never bland, just polished, lush and relaxed, with the Atlantic always close and the heights calling just behind.

(O) São Tiago Fortress; (L) Mist-covered mountain scenery; (T) Ivy-clad arches in Funchal; (B) Unique to Funchal – wicker basket toboggan rides down the hill

Azores (Ponta Delgada)

PORTUGAL

Ponta Delgada has a satisfyingly spacious seafront and a historic centre where character is woven into every street. It's not a glossy city, and that's part of the appeal. Faded façades and slightly time-warped bars sit alongside real architectural weight, with black-and-white basalt churches, arcaded squares, old convents, grand civic buildings and streets paved in patterned *calçada*. The town has a quietly atmospheric, mid-Atlantic texture, with harbour light, botanical gardens, café terraces and volcanic stone giving its worn edges a distinctive Azorean charm. It also works as a springboard for São Miguel's lush and volcanic interior, from crater lakes at Sete Cidades to Furnas's steaming fumaroles. Out on the water, whale-watching is central to the Azorean story, a striking reversal from the whaling era, with operators now bound by ethical guidelines.

(O) The historic entrance (Portas da Cidade) to the village of Ponta Delgada; (L) A pineapple plant in its first stage of growth; (T) View of Sete Cidades, near Miradouro da Grota do Inferno

Bilbao *SPAIN*

Bilbao's great trick is that it seldom feels like a big city, even though it stretches for kilometres along the Río Nervión with green slopes always visible beyond the skyline. Its modern identity is built on reinvention: the Guggenheim's arrival turned a post-industrial wasteland into a major draw and sparked broader redevelopment that made the city feel newly confident. Yet Bilbao still delivers on older pleasures too, especially in the Casco Viejo, a tight-knit maze of lanes and squares where the *pintxo* bars make grazing feel like a cultural obligation. Walk from the Casco Viejo towards the Guggenheim and the city's transformation unfolds in one stroll: medieval lanes, *pintxo* bars, bridges, riverside promenades and titanium curves, all held together by a place that feels ambitious without losing its everyday Basque pulse.

(L) The Guggenheim Museum; (T) Traditional Basque-style buildings in Casco Viejo; (B) Mouthwatering pintxos at a bar

Amsterdam *NETHERLANDS*

Amsterdam is engineered for lingering. Canals slow the pace of travel, gabled houses reward looking up, and neighbourhoods shift in mood from one bridge to the next. Water is the organizing principle here, not a backdrop, giving the city its rhythm, reflections and intimate sense of scale. The historic centre can feel busy, but the magic often lies slightly off the obvious routes, where canal-side cafés, small museums, quiet courtyards and handsome merchant houses restore its human texture. Amsterdam also does grand culture without pomposity: the Rijksmuseum, Van Gogh Museum and Anne Frank House carry real weight, while the bike-first rhythm keeps the city brisk, practical and lived-in. Instantly recognizable yet hard to exhaust, it is a place where wandering, pausing and following the water can feel as rewarding as any planned itinerary.

(O) NEMO Science Museum; (T) Canal boats ply the waterways; (B) Van Gogh's self-portrait in the Rijksmuseum

La Coruña/Santiago de Compostela *SPAIN*

Galicia feels fiercely Atlantic – green, wet, craggy and wind-whipped, with a coastline cut into deep *rías* and a culture that holds proudly to its own language, food and traditions. La Coruña gives that seaward identity an immediate focus, with beaches close to the centre, broad waterfront walks and the Torre de Hércules, a Roman-founded lighthouse still standing watch over the headland. Santiago de Compostela draws visitors inland without losing the sense of regional weather and stone. As the great medieval goal of the Camino, it carries memories of the centuries of pilgrimage in its arcaded streets, granite squares and worn approaches to the cathedral. The old core is a ravishing labyrinth, solemn in rain and golden in sudden sun. Together, La Coruña and Santiago demonstrate Galicia's distinctive character: Atlantic-facing, rain-polished, Celtic-tinged and anchored by its own language, cuisine and history.

(O) Santiago de Compostela's cathedral; (L) Preparing the famous huge botafumeiro swing in the cathedral; (T) Torre de Hercules in La Coruña

NATIONAL
PARK
SERVICE

Caribbean-Northern & Greater Antilles

Across the northern Caribbean and Greater Antilles, the sea shifts from glassy Bahamian shallows to reef-bright channels, deep harbours and mountain-backed island coasts. This is the Caribbean of old forts, pastel waterfronts, duty-free bustle, rum bars, reggae rhythms and beaches that seem almost theatrically blue. Between Spanish, Dutch, British, French and African influences, the region is sunny and accessible, but also rich in cultural variety.

Nassau *BAHAMAS*

(T) Vibrant houses on Nassau

Nassau is the Bahamas in miniature – a compact, walkable colonial core pressed up against a cruise-ship harbour, with Bay Street's bustle giving way fast to government squares, forts and sudden glimpses of turquoise beyond the buildings. The city's atmosphere comes from its Loyalist-era architecture and its earlier life as a pirate haunt, a history that still clings to the lanes around Rawson Square and Parliament Square. Step inland for a quick hit of elevation at Fort Fincastle and the Water Tower, then duck down the Queen's Staircase before the heat catches you. When you want to get back to the sea air, hop across to Paradise Island for wide Atlantic beaches, or head west to Cable Beach where casuarinas hiss over pale sand and the day ends in a long, easy sunset.

San Juan *PUERTO RICO*

San Juan brings the Caribbean into sharp historical focus. Salt air, street life and citadel walls are held together in one compact, walkable city. Old San Juan is one of the hemisphere's great colonial quarters, built as Spain's fortified Atlantic gateway and still defined by blue cobbles, pastel façades, wrought-iron balconies and the massive defences of El Morro and San Cristóbal. Yet the city is no preserved relic. Puerto Rico's African, Spanish and Taíno inheritances run through its food, music, language and festivals, while neighbourhoods beyond the old walls add beach life, contemporary restaurants and late-running bars. The best of San Juan lies in that range: a morning among ramparts and ocean views, an afternoon by the water, then an evening of *mofongo* (fried green plantains), salsa rhythms and streets that keep their colour after dark.

(L) Waves lap a San Juan beach; (T) Paseo de la Princesa in San Juan; (B) Local nightlife is lively

1671

St Thomas

US VIRGIN ISLANDS

St Thomas can be lively, even brash, but its appeal is rooted in how much the island gathers into a small radius. Charlotte Amalie curls around the harbour in red-roofed, whitewashed tiers, with old Danish warehouses now serving as galleries, boutiques and cafés, and street names such as Dronningens Gade and Kongens Gade still pointing to the island's colonial past. Duty-free shopping is popular, but the stronger rewards lie beyond the storefronts. Historic steps climb the hillsides, Fort Christian anchors the waterfront, and ferries, yachts and water taxis keep the harbour in constant motion. Beaches on the north and east coasts supply the other half of the island's appeal, from the broad sweep of Magens Bay to smaller coves where the water is intensely blue. A short journey beyond town reveals West Indian rhythms, sea-going life and steep green views all folded into this compact island.

(O) Fort Christian in Charlotte Amalie;
(L) Charlotte Amalie's harbour; (T) Local green iguana

Belgian
olate Box
Beatrix
Maarten
The Belgian Chocolate Box
By Beatrix
OPEN
BLAST
Clothes and gifts from Paris

Philipsburg

SINT MAARTEN/SAINT-MARTIN

Philipsburg is where Sint Maarten's dual identity comes into focus: a Dutch-side waterfront with a practical, upbeat energy, and the French cafés, markets and quieter lanes of Marigot only a short drive away. The island's easy contrasts are intriguing. It is compact but culturally split, polished in places yet informal in spirit, with serious beaches, lively restaurants and a confident taste for good living. Front Street gives Philipsburg its commercial bustle, while the boardwalk and Great Bay keep the sea close to the centre of town. Beyond it, the island opens quickly into a circuit of beaches and viewpoints. Maho is famous for aircraft skimming low over the sand, Orient Bay brings a broad, sociable sweep of beach life, and smaller coves offer calmer water and a slower pace. Philipsburg makes the island's variety feel unusually easy to grasp, with a working harbour, a busy waterfront, good beaches and two distinct cultures all packed into a small, accessible place.

(L) A vintage ride on the streets of Philipsburg, Sint Maarten

George Town

CAYMAN ISLANDS

George Town is Cayman's busy front porch, a small harbour town that comes alive when the tenders start running and duty-free windows begin to glitter. It can feel polished, even a touch corporate, yet the appeal is how quickly you can pivot from pavements to water. Downtown's compact sights include the Cayman Islands National Museum in its 180-year-old former courthouse, plus a short loop past the upturned-hull ceiling of Elmslie Memorial Church and the murals and monuments of Heroes Square. The real reason to dock here, though, is offshore: gin-clear seas, dramatic walls and caverns, and boat trips to Stingray City where rays glide through shallow water like they own the place. Finish with a swim or a stroll on Seven Mile Beach, only minutes away, and the island's easy, sunlit logic clicks into place.

(O) A cruise tender docked by the pier in modern George Town; (L) Fresh snapper for sale; (T) Heroes Square; (B) Historic shops downtown

Jamaica (Montego Bay/ Ocho Rios) *JAMAICA*

Jamaica announces itself with colour, rhythm and confidence: music spilling from bars and taxis, vivid roadside signs, jerk smoke in the air and hills rising sharply behind the coast. Montego Bay and Ocho Rios are among the island's most accessible gateways, but their real value is how quickly they lead into a broader Jamaican landscape of beaches, rivers, gardens and deep green interior. Around Ocho Rios, waterfalls and forested slopes bring the island's lushness into focus, while Montego Bay offers broad sand, lively resorts and easy access to hillside viewpoints and local food stops. Food is central to the experience, from jerk chicken and patties to peppery sauces, rum and fresh fruit. Jamaica entices with personality, not polished uniformity: a bold, musical, generous, sometimes hectic vibe, rooted in a culture that has shaped the world far beyond its shores.

(O) Dunes River Falls near Ocho Rios; (L) Upmarket hotels and yachts in Montego Bay; (T) Montego Bay beach

Caribbean - Eastern & Southern

Across the eastern and southern Caribbean, the islands grow greener, more volcanic and varied, with coral-ringed bays, rainforested peaks, sugar-era towns and trade-wind coasts shaped by Atlantic swell. This is the Caribbean of plantation history, Creole flavours, rum shops, Dutch colour, British harbours and French-inflected ease. From beaches to wild interiors, the region feels lush, warm and richly layered, with each island carrying its own vivid rhythm.

MERRY CHRISTMAS

Bridgetown

BARBADOS

Bridgetown is a Caribbean capital with substance, merging British-colonial echoes, Bajan confidence and a waterfront that keeps pulling you back. Cruise ships dock just north of town, so it's easy to drop straight into the action, whether that means museums, rum-shop culture or simply letting the city's streets lead you towards the sea. Barbados has the beaches, of course, but what sets it apart is how much else it offers – plantation houses, caves, gullies and a proud cultural mix that shows up in everything from cricket to calypso. Bridgetown is the best quick introduction to that wider island character, lively without being overwhelming and well placed for a dash out to the coast when you want white sand and bright water to finish the day.

(L) Bridgetown's harbour

Castries ST LUCIA

Castries is often the starting point rather than the whole story when visiting St Lucia, but that is part of its value. The capital sits in a tight bowl of hills, with Morne Fortune rising above the harbour and giving the city a sense of drama before St Lucia's wilder scenery takes over. From the heights, the view draws together the island's essentials: blue water, steep green slopes, a busy working port and roads curling inland. The town itself has market bustle, colonial traces and a local energy that feels very different from the island's resort coast. Most visits soon reach beyond Castries, whether towards Marigot Bay, the rainforest interior, volcanic Soufrière or the Pitons rising from the south-west coast, but that range is what makes the capital such a useful gateway. It offers an immediate glimpse of St Lucian daily life, then opens quickly onto the landscapes that give the island its worldwide pull.

(O) Taking in the view of the Pitons; (T) Carnival time in Castries; (B) Marigot Bay is a great place for water-bound activities

St John's

ANTIGUA & BARBUDA

St John's is Antigua's charismatic front door, a compact capital where quays, markets and bars make it easy to fall straight into island tempo. Antigua's reputation rests on beaches, and rightly so, but the island's deeper interest lies in the contrast between polished holiday vibes and the physical traces of the sugar era that still mark the landscape. St John's gives that wider picture quickly. The National Museum adds context in the old courthouse, while the harbour, market stalls and colourful streets keep the town busy and practical rather than purely picturesque. From here, the island opens easily: west and north to calm beaches, south to English Harbour, Nelson's Dockyard and Shirley Heights, where Georgian naval history meets one of the Caribbean's great views. Even a short wander in St John's catches Antigua's essential mix of sociability, maritime history and everyday island life.

(O) Myriad architectural styles overlook St John's quay; (L) A British remnant; (T) Nelson's Dockyard, English Harbour; (B) Sunset view from St John's

Oranjestad *ARUBA*

(T) Dutch-style façades in Oranjestad

Oranjestad is Aruba's easy, harbourside capital, possessed of a bright Dutch-Caribbean sheen, and it's possible to wander past pastel façades, shopping streets, casinos, cafés and a compact downtown with great ease. Some of the architecture leans heavily into island fantasy, but Fort Zoutman and the King Willem III Tower give the centre a firmer historical anchor, recalling Aruba's earlier role as a small colonial outpost. The waterfront is the natural starting point, before the streets lead inland towards the fort's museum, shaded corners and tram-lined avenues. Oranjestad's strongest card, though, is proximity. A short journey north reveals the famous beach strip between Eagle and Palm beaches, where fine white sand and calm turquoise water explain Aruba's enduring popularity. The island can feel glossy, but Oranjestad delivers a clear, accessible version of its appeal: warm water, Dutch-Caribbean colour, easy urban pleasures and close-by beaches.

Willemstad *CURAÇAO*

Willemstad is the ABC islands' showstopper, a capital whose Dutch colonial architecture has earned UNESCO World Heritage status and whose colour feels anything but ornamental. Set around a working harbour, the city has a waterfront that rewards repeated crossings, especially when the light catches the gabled façades of Punda and the Queen Emma Bridge swings open for passing ships. Otrobanda gives the city a more residential counterpoint, with restored mansions, murals, courtyards and harbour views, while Pietermaai adds another layer of style and texture through crumbling façades, boutique hotels, bars and restaurants set inside old townhouses. Curaçao feels less polished than Aruba and less beach-resort driven than Bonaire, which gives Willemstad more urban interest. Beyond the capital, the island's smaller beaches bring extra range, from clear-water coves on the west coast to easy swimming closer to town.

(O) Candy-coloured homes in Pietermaai; (T) Primary colours abound in Willemstad; (B) Idyllic shores at Cas Abao beach

Roseau

DOMINICA

Roseau is small, scruffy and full of atmosphere, a Caribbean capital that hasn't been buffed into blandness. One moment you're on the tidy Bay Front promenade, the next you're threading narrow streets lined with ramshackle wooden houses, louvred windows and sagging French-style balconies held up on stilts. It's easy to cover on foot, which is part of the pleasure: visit the museum for quick context, delve into the markets for noise and colour, then take a steep pull up Morne Bruce for a view that reminds you Dominica is a volcanic mountain masquerading as an island. Roseau is also a launch pad for what makes Dominica special, experiences such as snorkelling bubbles at Champagne Beach, serious diving around Scotts Head, and rainforest hikes that lead to waterfalls, gorges and the island's brooding Boiling Lake.

(O) Dancer at the Dominica Carnival; (L) The island's cruise port terminal; (T) Scott's Head

North America Atlantic & Gulf Coast

Along North America's Atlantic and Gulf edges, the mood shifts from big-city drama to sea-air villages, French-walled streets, Lowcountry grace and tropical irreverence. This is a coast that runs the gamut from iconic skylines to lighthouses, autumn forests, maritime memory, jazz, seafood and river-mouth heat, where old ports still carry the energy of arrival and departure. Varied, storied and atmospheric, it reveals a continent shaped powerfully by water.

New York City *USA*

(T) Brookyn Bridge framed by Downtown Manhattan

New York makes its first impression at full volume: skyline, river traffic, bridges and towers, all carrying the sense of a city already several moves ahead. Its power lies in the layering. Wall Street's narrow canyons, Lower East Side tenements, cast-iron SoHo, brownstone Brooklyn and midtown's clean vertical thrust each reveal a different version of the city. The landmarks are impossible to ignore – Times Square, the Rockefeller Center, the Empire State Building, Central Park, the Statue of Liberty – but New York is more than a checklist of icons. Its charge comes from the mix of languages, the food carts and galleries, the subway rumble, the sudden pocket park, and the block-by-block shifts in mood and architecture. The waterfront and big green spaces give the density room to breathe, while the city's cultural life makes it feel perpetually unfinished. Historic, restless, crowded and creative, New York City is impossible to reduce to a single view.

Boston *USA*

Boston is the rare American city that wears its history without feeling stuck in it. The colonial past is right there in the street plan and the brick-and-stone dignity, yet the place stays lively thanks to its world-beating universities, restaurants, and a famous waterfront that's enjoyable to explore. It's also compact enough to work beautifully as a port call: start around Boston Common and the Public Garden, then follow the Freedom Trail's red-brick line through the city's defining chapters. Between stops you get neighbourhood character for free, from Beacon Hill's sophistication to the North End's narrow streets and Italian-American appetite. Boston is both elegant and earthy, but emminently usable; a city you can genuinely get to know in a day, and still leave with the itch to return for longer.

(L) Beacon Hill; (T) Boston's modern skyline; (B) Aboard a swan boat in Boston Public Garden

Bar Harbor *MAINE, USA*

Bar Harbor sits neatly between small-town harbour life and Acadia's granite wildness. Maine's coast is famously "drowned", a crumpled edge of coves, islands and peninsulas where land and sea keep interrupting one another, and Bar Harbor makes a handsome base in that landscape. The town itself is walkable and breezy, with shingled houses, working boats, seafood restaurants and views across Frenchman Bay. The stronger pull lies just beyond town on Mount Desert Island, where Acadia National Park gathers much of coastal Maine's drama into a compact, accessible landscape. Forested slopes climb to pink-granite cliffs, carriage roads thread through the woods, and viewpoints such as Cadillac Mountain and Thunder Hole bring the Atlantic into sharp focus. Even a short visit can take in harbour streets, lobster rolls, spruce-scented paths and surf breaking against stone. Bar Harbor gives Maine a clear shape – maritime, outdoorsy, well kept and edged by genuine wildness.

(O) Bar Harbor's quaint shopping street; (T) A lobster boat heading out at dawn; (B) Buoys acting as decoration

HALIFAX HARBOUR TOURS

Halifax

NOVA SCOTIA, CANADA

Halifax is one of those ports that makes sense the instant you see the harbour: broad water, a working waterfront turned strollable, and a city that still feels shaped by the sea. It grew into its modern role after World War II, becoming the Maritimes' financial and educational hub, but the older identity lingers in the Citadel above downtown and the naval-town backbone that never really left. The centre is compact and lively, with students, street performers and a slightly scruffy creative edge balancing the city's commercial confidence. On a short visit, Halifax is a hit because the good stuff clusters close together: museums and historic buildings tucked below the fortress, then the Waterfront Boardwalk linking shops, sights and sea air without the hassle of traffic.

(O) Hanging out on Halifax Waterfront Boardwalk; (L) Fresh lobster at the fisherman's market; (T) Macdonald Bridge

Quebec City

CANADA

Québec City is the rare North American place that can genuinely make you forget the continent you're on. Vieux-Québec is the only walled city in North America, a maze of cobbled streets and stone buildings that feels profoundly French-Canadian rather than merely historic. The setting does half the work: Cap Diamant rising over the narrowing St Lawrence, with the Château Frontenac perched like a storybook provocation above the river. Cruise ships come here for the romance, and they get it, but the city's appeal runs deeper than photogenic streets. It's a working provincial capital with a strong Francophone identity, where cafés, museums and public squares sit naturally among the fortifications. Even a simple stroll from Haute-Ville down to Basse-Ville delivers that satisfying sense of distinct place.

(L) Château Frontenac looms above its neighbouring buildings

Charleston

SOUTH CAROLINA, USA

Charleston is a city of beautiful surfaces with a sharp history underneath, a tension that makes it compelling. The old houses, ironwork, church steeples and hidden gardens are undeniably handsome, but they are best seen with an awareness of what built them, and how deeply the city's story is tied to slavery, trade, secession and the wider South. The historic core is richly walkable, with cobbled lanes, piazza-fronted houses, museums and a harbour edge that keeps drawing the eye back to the water. House tours here are not just architecture-as-pretty-object; at their best, they open doors onto lives, labour, power and the city's long, complicated past. Fort Sumter, the Battery and the Old Slave Mart Museum add essential context, while excellent food, a strong arts scene and humid coastal light give Charleston its present-day pull. It is a place of grace and reckoning, where beauty is more interesting because it cannot be separated from history.

(O) French Quarter, Charleston; (L) Sunset over the Ashley River; (T) The campus clock at the College of Charleston; (B) Travelling the traditional way

New Orleans

LOUISIANA, USA

New Orleans remains defiantly itself, a city shaped by a dense mix of French, Spanish, African, Caribbean and American influences. Its beauty is also inseparable from its fragility. Filigree balconies, fern-hung courtyards, above-ground cemeteries and weathered shutters all speak to a place built on low ground and always alert to heat, water and decay. The French Quarter remains the obvious starting point, with its ironwork, bars, restaurants and battered grandeur, but the city's range extends well beyond Bourbon Street. Tremé carries deep musical weight and the riverfront keeps the Mississippi firmly in view. Food is one of the city's great forms of storytelling, from gumbo and po'boys to oysters and beignets. After Hurricane Katrina, New Orleans' resilience became part of its modern story, but its pull lies in a street-level culture of brass bands, late nights, strong flavours and public celebration.

(O) French Quarter architecture; (L) Tradtional riverboat travel on the Mississippi; (T) A jazz band performing in the French Quarter

Key West *FLORIDA, USA*

Key West feels like the end of the map, and it trades shamelessly on that aura of salt-stained freedom. The Overseas Highway sets the scene as a long, bright run over water, but the real payoff is the town itself: Caribbean-leaning architecture, a famously raucous nightlife, and a creative streak that has long attracted writers and misfits. Key West isn't a classic beach resort, and that's part of its appeal. You come for sunsets, for bars that know how to host, for museums and old homes that hint at a surprisingly rich past, and for the sense that the island has always been slightly apart from the mainland. Wander Old Town's leafy lanes, dip into Bahama Village for an older Key West feel, then end where everyone ends up: facing west, watching the sky turn molten over the water.

(L) Key West Lighthouse; (T) Pathway to the ocean; (B) Brown pelicans waiting for fish at Robbie's Marina

Alaska

Along Alaska's southern coast, the scale turns immense, with tidewater glaciers, blue-white ice, forested fjords and mountains rising straight from cold, wildlife-rich water. The USA's northernmost state offers gold-rush stories, Indigenous heritage, salmon rivers, harbour towns and national parks where the landscape still feels thrillingly in charge. Mist, snow peaks and sudden shafts of light give every view a sense of drama and raw northern beauty.

YEIL
TRAM

Juneau *ALASKA, USA*

Alaska's capital feels improbably lively for a place hemmed in by mountains and sea. Downtown is compact and busy, with narrow streets and alleys slipping between museums, galleries and bars, yet wilderness is never more than a short walk or ride away. The city began with a gold strike in 1880, but its real modern rhythm comes from people grabbing the clear days when they appear, sometimes closing shop simply to get outside. Head for Douglas Island for a quieter, local mood and a web of trails, or point yourself towards the Mendenhall Glacier, where a frigid lake collects freshly calved ice and the great Juneau Icefield looms beyond. For a final toast, the Alaska Brewing Company offers tastings that suit the climate.

(L) Taking the Goldbelt tram, which departs from near the cruise terminal, and whisks passengers 1,800 feet up the side of Mount Roberts

Glacier Bay *ALASKA, USA*

(T) Taking a boat tour in Glacier Bay

If Alaska has a grandstand, Glacier Bay is it: a vast sweep of fjords and ice where the scenery refuses to sit still. The park and preserve covers 3.3 million acres, straddling climates from marine to Arctic, so the wildlife checklist is as dramatic as the geology. Cruise ships come for the main event, which is the spectacle of the tidewater glaciers pouring down from the Fairweather Range and dropping into the bay with the crack and thunder of calving ice. Between those blue-white walls you're in a world of icebergs and scoured rock, then suddenly saltwater beaches, quiet coves, freshwater lakes and forests of western hemlock and Sitka spruce. Humpbacks, seals, bears and eagles are all part of the appeal, but the real hook is the feeling of travelling through a shifting landscape.

Skagway *ALASKA, USA*

Skagway sells its past with a wink, yet the place still carries the restless charge of the Klondike. In 1897–98 the stampeders arrived and a boomtown of up to 20,000 people sprang up at the head of the Inside Passage, framed by steep mountains rising straight out of a saltwater fjord. Today, Broadway's preserved false fronts and boardwalks recreate the noise and bravado for cruise-day crowds, but it's not just a costume show – the town is a genuine gateway over the coastal range into the Yukon, and even the steep trail to Upper Dewey Lake gives a sudden, lung-opening taste of the wild country pressing in above the rooftops. The definitive way to understand that ambition is to take the White Pass and Yukon Route Railway, a narrow-gauge engineering marvel done easily as a day excursion, that claws up the mountainside towards White Pass Summit, with the old trails still visible far below.

(L) Skagway comes alive in summer; (T) A train on the White Pass and Yukon Route Railway; (B) Upper Dewey Lake

Seward (Kenai Fjords)

ALASKA, USA

Seward is small, attractive and sea-minded, set on Resurrection Bay with a working port energy that suits its role as a cruise terminus. The town was founded in 1903, took a hit in the 1964 earthquake, then found its feet again, and it now thrives on being the front door to the Kenai Fjords. Out on the water, wildlife cruises push into rugged coastal fjords where glaciers are the headline act – Holgate Glacier is a favourite, calving into a deep, still fjord with a theatrical crack and boom – and the supporting cast includes sea otters, sea lions, porpoises and whales, plus puffins and bald eagles wheeling overhead. Back on land, the Alaska SeaLife Center adds a thoughtful counterpoint, combining research with rehabilitation of injured birds and mammals. For a quick, satisfying taste of ice without a boat, Exit Glacier is a straightforward trail walk to the edge of the Harding Icefield.

(O) Kayakers watch falling icebergs at Holgate Glacier; (L) Freshly-caught fish hung up at Seward's docks; (T) Seward's small harbour; (B) A local puffin pair

Mexico, Central America & Colombia

Between Mexico, Central America and Colombia, the tropics feel bold, vivid and wonderfully varied. Coral reefs, desert arches, jungle coasts, colonial balconies and one of the world's great engineered passages combine to heady effect. Here, Mayan traces, Garifuna rhythms, Mexican resort energy, Caribbean colour and Spanish-walled grandeur sit close to rainforests and reef-bright water, in a region of heat, history and spectacle, with adventure never far inland.

Cozumel *MEXICO*

(T) Diving over coral in Cozumel

Cozumel has long been familiar territory for cruise passengers, but it still makes a strong case for lingering. San Miguel, the island's only town, lines its *malecón* with the expected mix of restaurants, bars and souvenir storefronts, yet a few blocks inland the gloss drops away and the pace becomes more local. The island's real treasure lies offshore. Its reefs – made famous internationally by Jacques Cousteau – remain among the finest in the Caribbean, with clear water, bright coral and easy drift snorkelling that can turn even a short outing into something memorable. Away from the built-up southwest coast, Cozumel quickly becomes quieter and greener, with Maya ruins at San Gervasio, low forest once associated with the island's name as the "land of the swallows", and a windward eastern shore of surf, beach shacks and empty horizons. It is too popular to feel undiscovered, but the best of Cozumel is still elemental – reef, road, wind and water.

Cabo San Lucas *MEXICO*

Cabo San Lucas sits at the very tip of the Baja California peninsula, where the Sea of Cortez gives way to the Pacific – that meeting of waters explains much of its drama. The marina and nightlife are brash, busy and built for pleasure, but the natural setting keeps the place from becoming just another resort town. Playa El Médano is the practical beach – broad, sociable and usually calm enough for swimming, with the crowds thinning as you walk away from the densest run of bars and restaurants. From there, water taxis run out towards Land's End, where granite formations rise in sculptural shapes from the sea and frame the small, sheltered curve of Playa del Amor. A few steps away, Playa Divorcio faces the Pacific with an entirely different temperament: beautiful, exposed and unsafe for swimming, its surf and undertow making the contrast brutally clear. Cabo's enduring image is El Arco, the natural stone arch carved at the peninsula's end, where boats pause between sea-lion rocks, turquoise shallows and the darker blue of open ocean.

(L) Super-yachts moored up; (T) El Arco, where the Pacific meets the Sea of Cortez; (B) Playa El Médano

Puerto Vallarta

MEXICO

Puerto Vallarta manages to feel like a resort without losing its sense of place. It's certainly commercial (and knows how to party), but its core still has the shape of a town, with cobbled streets fanning out from a colonial plaza above an oceanfront boulevard. The wider Bahía de Banderas is the prime destination, offering warm, tropical beach life with enough variety to suit a day ashore, from quick swims near town to boat hops down the coast. Offshore, humpback whales turn up seasonally, giving winter cruises a bonus spectacle. Venture beyond the downtown strands and the coast starts breaking into coves backed by forested mountains, the kind of landscape that makes you understand why this stretch of Mexico's Pacific has always lured travellers northward, chasing sunsets and seafood, with the sea breeze in their face.

(O) Los Muertos pier, with its central metal structure uniquely designed to resemble a ship's billowing sail; (L) Palms on Bahía de Banderas; (T) A glimpse of a humpback whale

JAMES BRODIE & CO LTD

Belize City *BELIZE*

Belize City is messy, vital and, for most travellers, unavoidable: the transport hub where you regroup before scattering to the cayes or heading inland. It isn't polished, but it gives an honest first taste of Belize's distinctive blend – officially English-speaking, Caribbean in rhythm, and blending Maya, Mestizo, African and European elements. Its value lies less in grand monuments than in its position at the hinge of the country. Offshore lie the reef and cayes that define Belize's daydream image, with the Great Blue Hole reachable on a scenic flight for those who want the country's most famous natural icon in a single, startling glance; inland, the roads lead quickly towards caves, rainforest and ruined Maya cities. Even a short stay can justify a detour to the Belize Zoo, which offers a vivid close-up view of rehabilitated jaguars, tapirs, scarlet macaws and other wildlife most visitors otherwise glimpse only in brochures.

(L) Belize City at sunset; (T) Cerros Mayan Ruins; (B) The Great Blue Hole on the Belize Barrier Reef

Roatán

HONDURAS

Roatán can look like a simple beach-and-dive stop, but it's an island with distinct corners and moods. West End is the easy favourite, with calm water, a sheltered curve of sand at Half Moon Bay and a sandy track lined with guesthouses, bars and dive shops. Further on, West Bay delivers the postcard version, a white-sand beach under coconut palms with clear water and easy reef snorkelling, though it's also where the crowds land hardest. For a quieter swim, Sandy Bay has a more lived-in feel and access to the reef without West Bay's gloss, while Camp Bay, far to the east, is the island's wilder beach escape. Away from the west, Roatán turns more workaday and interesting, from the fishing port of French Harbour to Oak Ridge's harbour-front wooden houses and mangrove trips. For a cultural pivot, Punta Gorda is Roatán's oldest Garífuna community, adding a deeper note to the island.

(O) Coxen Hole, the capital of Roatán; (L) A perfect frame at a pier entrance at Sandy Bay; (T) An over-water bar at West Bay Beach

Cartagena

COLOMBIA

Cartagena is a city to explore slowly, preferably on foot and with no great faith in the map. Start inside the thick colonial walls, where the old town folds together balconies and bougainvillea, carved doors, shaded plazas, boutique hotels and restaurants that turn candlelit after dark. It is romantic, but punchy – expensive mansions sit close to beer shops, fruit sellers and ceviche carts, and the heat keeps everything loose around the edges. Just beyond the walls, Getsemaní gives the city a sharper pulse, with murals, music, domino games and plazas that feel functional rather than preserved. Walk up to Castillo San Felipe de Barajas for the scale of the old Spanish fortress system, then return to the sea-facing battlements towards sunset, when the walls catch the light and the modern towers of Bocagrande remind you that Cartagena is still changing. The literary associations are real – Gabriel García Márquez loved the place – but the city does not need borrowing from fiction. Its best moments are small and immediate – a doorway, a drumbeat, a sudden square, the smell of frying *arepas* in the heat.

(L) Cathedral Santa Catalina de Alejandría in colonial Cartagena

Panama Canal (Colón/Balboa) *PANAMA*

The Panama Canal is pure scale and precision, an 80km slash across the isthmus that still feels like a dare. The best way to experience it is from the deck of a ship, taking in the drama that is in the contrast: gargantuan vessels manoeuvred with surprising delicacy, while jungle presses close to the banks and little forested islands drift by in Lago Gatún. A transit, even a partial one, turns the canal from abstract marvel into lived experience, travelling under the Bridge of the Americas, through the tight Culebra Cut, and in the slow, inevitable lift and drop of lock chambers at Miraflores and Pedro Miguel. It's engineering as theatre, with rainforest as the backdrop. If you stay on deck, you'll also notice how the canal corridor is not a sterile industrial zone but a green, protected strip for much of its length, which only adds to the sense of improbable achievement.

(O) The Panama Canal from above; (L) Panama City's ultra-modern towers; (T) The Bridge of the Americas; (B) A cruise ship traverses the Panama Canal

South America

Around South America, the sea reveals a continent of extremes, from samba-bright beaches to grand river cities, wind-scoured ports to glacier-cut channels, and islands where wildlife appears to have kept its own calendar. The journey can move from tropical idyll to Patagonian emptiness, from cosmopolitan waterfronts and painted hillsides to black water, blue ice and volcanic shorelines. Few regions offer such a sense of scale, or such thrillingly abrupt variety.

Rio de Janeiro *BRAZIL*

(T) The iconic sweep of Copacabana beach

Rio is the rare city that looks like a film set and still lives up to its reputation. *Cariocas* (residents of the city) call it the "Cidade Maravilhosa", and the case is made by the skyline alone: Sugar Loaf at the mouth of Guanabara Bay, Corcovado crowned by *Christ the Redeemer,* and the long, famous sweeps of Copacabana and Ipanema where the beach doubles as the city's main social club. The setting is almost indecently beautiful, a 20km strip between sea and forest-clad mountains, dotted with islands and framed by peaks. Add Carnaval's sensory overload, the nightlife of districts like Lapa, and the easy escape into Tijuca's urban rainforest, and you have a destination that earns its iconic status on the daily. Rio's inequalities and development pressures are undeniable, but they don't erase the essential allure of this astonishing bay-side metropolis.

Buenos Aires *ARGENTINA*

Buenos Aires is a capital with a hundred nicknames and one core talent: it seduces. Grand and eclectic, European-influenced yet unmistakably itself, it's a place of late dinners, crowded cafés and a cultural calendar that barely pauses. Tango and football aren't just attractions but living obsessions, while *mate* rituals play out in parks and plazas shaded by trees. The city's scale can look intimidating, yet much of what you'll want is concentrated in a handful of barrios: historic streets and antiques in San Telmo, colour and swagger in La Boca, French-style palaces in Retiro and Recoleta, and the fashionable sprawl of Palermo's shops and restaurants. Along the caramel-coloured Río de la Plata, the port and cruise terminal underscore its outward-looking energy. Buenos Aires rarely behaves like a simple tableau; it feels like a city that expects you to keep up with its rhythm.

(L) Congreso Nacional (T) Caminito open-air museum in La Boca; (B) Tango is ever-present in Buenos Aires

Montevideo

URUGUAY

Montevideo has the confidence of a capital that doesn't need to raise its voice. Uruguay's main gateway is best taken slowly, with the rambla tracing the Río de la Plata for miles and turning the waterfront into a shared living room for walkers, cyclists, *mate*-drinkers and sunset watchers. That easy rhythm is central to the city's appeal, but it should not be mistaken for sleepiness. Montevideo has serious cultural weight, from the old streets and market halls of Ciudad Vieja to tango, theatre, football and a nightlife scene that gathers pace after dark. It also sits neatly between worlds: close enough to Buenos Aires to feel part of the same fabric, yet calmer, smaller and distinctly Uruguayan. Add ferries, beaches and day trips to colonial towns, and the city becomes more than a soft landing in the region, but a poised, quietly charismatic capital, worth visiting in its own right.

(O) Historic architecture downtown; (L) Las Llamadas festival participant; (T) Montevideo is situated on the banks of the Río de la Plata; (B) Fishing boats in Puerto del Buceo

Ushuaia *ARGENTINA*

Ushuaia trades heavily on its "end of the world" status, and for once the slogan seems pretty reasonable. The city is wedged between the last jagged folds of the Andes and the Beagle Channel, so even arriving feels dramatic. It's a year-round resort and a working port, with boats heading out into a cold, stunning waterway rich in wildlife, and with Parque Nacional Tierra del Fuego close enough for easy hikes through forests, lakes and tundra. The appeal is the combination of accessibility and rawness: you can be eating fresh *centolla* in town one moment and bouncing across slate-grey water the next, scanning for sea lions and birds. Ushuaia also has the forward-looking feel of a jumping-off point, whether that means exploring deeper into the archipelago or simply getting your passport stamped for the bragging rights. Few ports feel so convincingly remote.

(L) Ushuaia's dramatic waterfront landscape; (T) Sea lions in the Beagle Channel; (B) The Post Office at the End of the World

Punta Arenas

CHILE

Punta Arenas sits on the Magellan Strait like a stubborn outpost that decided to become a city. From above it's a patchwork of tin roofs and brightly painted houses climbing from the water, with grand nineteenth-century mansions from the wool-boom era still holding their ground beside modern offices. The wind is really part of the city's personality, sharpening the views from lookouts like Mirador Cerro la Cruz and giving the sea a perpetually restless look. Historically it was fuelled by maritime traffic and sheep ranching, and it still feels like a place built around movement, whether that's travellers heading for Tierra del Fuego, or the enduring pull of Antarctica-bound routes. Lean into the strait's wildlife and history with boat trips to Isla Magdalena's huge Magellanic penguin colony, or drives south to the bleak story of Puerto Hambre. Punta Arenas is a compelling frontier city, weather-whipped and transient.

(O) "Monument to the Crew of the Schooner Ancud" in Punta Arenas; (L) Clock tower overlooking the city; (B) A Magellanic penguin chick on Isla Magdalena

Chilean Fjords *CHILE*

(T) Early morning over the Chilean fjords

The Chilean fjords are Patagonia in its most elemental form, where the Andes take their last dramatic breath and plunge into the ocean, breaking the coast into channels, islands and storm-battered inlets. This is a landscape defined by water and weather: persistent winds, short summers, and mountains that seem to rise straight out of steel-grey sea. The human history feels just as stark, shaped by Indigenous seafarers who knew these frigid passages intimately, and by later explorers who mapped and named straits and sounds on the way to somewhere else. For cruise travellers, the seduction is the daily shifting scenery: peaks and glaciers in the distance, sudden waterfalls, and long stretches where the only obvious signs of life are seabirds and the occasional marine mammal breaking the surface. It's not about ticking off sights but letting the coastline's wild geometry do the work.

Valparaíso *CHILE*

Valparaíso is Chile's most intriguing city, a mad amphitheatre of hills around a wide bay, with colourful houses tumbling down towards a narrow strip of lower town. It can feel rough-edged, even moth-eaten in places, yet that's part of the spell – a working port with a romantic, crumbling beauty that rewards curiosity. The city's secret weapon is verticality. The antiquated *ascensores*, funicular lifts built in the late nineteenth and early twentieth centuries, haul you up to viewpoints and into hilltop neighbourhoods where the best wandering begins. Cerros Alegre and Concepción are a maze of steep lanes, elegant mansions and bright paintwork, shaped by immigrant fortunes and still good for lingering over the view as the lights flicker on across the bay. Down below, the port district has its own grit and character, but Valparaíso's real magic is the moment you crest a hill and the whole city opens out beneath you.

(L) Eccentric, colourful houses in Valparaíso; (T) The city's streets ascend the hills; (B) Street art in the city

Galápagos Islands *ECUADOR*

The Galápagos are one of the few destinations that feel genuinely world-changing. Thirteen stark volcanic islands and a scatter of islets sit far out in the Pacific, and their strange, uncompromising landscapes helped spark Darwin's thinking on evolution. Today, the draw is the fearless wildlife, which makes encounters feel unusually intimate: sea lions drifting past your mask, boobies performing their absurd courtship routines, marine iguanas piled like prehistoric sculpture on black lava. The islands are tightly managed, with most land protected as a national park and visitors funnelled to designated sites, which keeps the experience focused on what matters. Cruise-style itineraries suit the archipelago perfectly, letting you wake each day in a different ecosystem, from white beaches to cactus-studded slopes and misty highlands. What stays with you is the rare sensation of entering a living laboratory, where nature is not scenery but the central force.

(L) A marine iguana and blue footed boobies, some of the Galápagos' celebrated wildlife

Asia

Across Asia, the sea opens onto dazzling contrasts – a mix of vertical skylines, limestone bays, lantern-lit old towns, temple capitals, tropical islands and reefs of almost unreal colour. Here, ancient trade routes meet hyper-modern cities, while jungle, volcano, karst and coral give the region immense physical drama. From Southeast Asian heat to Japanese refinement, the ports here offer a vast, varied, vivid spectacle of movement and flavour.

Singapore

SINGAPORE

Compact but crammed with swagger, Singapore is one of the great cruise stopovers. This small island nation punches far above its weight, with a port that helped turn it from colonial outpost into modern metropolis. Far from a sterile "Asia-lite", Singapore's dazzling architectural ambition and distinct neighbourhoods make it a delight for visitors. At street level, it's fun to explore these enclaves, from Little India and Arab Street to Chinatown and the Civic District. Come hungry: eating is a national sport, and the city's mix of Chinese, Malay and Indian cultures plays out most deliciously in hawker centres and high-end kitchens alike. When you want a breather, Singapore's "garden" side appears in surprisingly lush green zones and big-ticket attractions that feel improbably serene for a hyper-organized city-state.

(L) The dazzling Gardens by the Bay

Hong Kong *HONG KONG*

Hong Kong is always best approached by water, with its evocative skyline of high-rise bravado rising straight from Victoria Harbour and ferries connecting island to mainland with a sense of everyday theatre. Between the harbourfront shimmer and the steep hills behind it, the city's energy is immediate and unapologetic, from the frenzy of shopping districts to late-night scenes in Lan Kwai Fong. It's also a place to slow down with purpose, ideally over *yum cha*, where dim sum and fragrant tea deliver Cantonese culture in bite-sized form. When the pace gets too sharp, escape to parks and viewpoints that remind you how much green still clings to the city's slopes. Hong Kong doesn't do subtle, but it does do unforgettable.

(L) Victoria Peak's famous green tram ascends to the observation deck; (T) Victoria Harbour at sunset; (B) Nan Lian Garden

Ha Long Bay

VIETNAM

Ha Long Bay earns its fame the moment you leave the shore behind and enter the maze of limestone towers that rise sheer from green water. Ridges fold like dragon backs, coves hide behind rock walls and caves open suddenly out of shadow. The great pleasure is not a single viewpoint but the slow rearranging of the landscape as a smaller boat threads between the karsts, making the bay feel at once vast and enclosed. On longer stays, an overnight junk gives the place its best chance to breathe, with dusk softening the cliffs into silhouettes and early morning returning a little of the stillness that first made Ha Long feel mythical. The crowds are real, but Cat Ba Island makes the best quieter counterpoint, with boats slipping quickly into Lan Ha Bay's limestone maze and the island itself adding beaches, forested hills and a more independent base for exploring the wider seascape. Wherever you land, the region is most powerful close to the water, where it feels like a mysterious otherworld.

(O) Sailing between the karsts; (L) A floating fishing village; (T) A monkey surveys the scene on Cat Ba Island; (B) Entering the port on Cat Ba Island

Da Nang (Hoi An) *VIETNAM*

Central Vietnam gathers an improbable amount into a short coastal stretch, with Da Nang and Hoi An making a natural pair. Hoi An is the heart-stealer: a compact old trading town of timber merchant houses, tiled roofs, Chinese assembly halls and the Japanese Covered Bridge, all threaded along the Thu Bon River. After dark, lanterns soften the streets around the old town and boats drift past with coloured lights on the water, but the place is strongest before the evening crowds build, when the markets, temples and shopfronts still feel lived-in. Da Nang is the sharper, faster counterpoint: a beach city of bridges, high-rises and seafood restaurants. Just outside the city, the Marble Mountains rise abruptly from the plain, with caves, pagodas and views back towards the coast, while the Cham Museum gives a more grounded sense of the region's older history. In the hills above Da Nang, Ba Na Hills adds a stranger, showier layer: a mountaintop resort reached by cable car, best known for the Golden Bridge held aloft by giant stone hands.

(O) The Japanese Covered Bridge in Hoi An old town; (T) Traditional lanterns lit up; (B) Walking over the Golden Bridge

Bangkok (Laem Chabang) *THAILAND*

Bangkok is a glorious assault on the senses: a vast, flat metropolis spiked with modern towers, yet still threaded with hushed golden temples and the river life that keeps the city breathing. The Chao Phraya is the spine, and the canals of Thonburi offer a glimpse of the amphibious Bangkok that once floated on water rather than traffic. For first-timers, the cultural gravity is irresistible, with the Grand Palace and Wat Phra Kaeo dazzling in the old royal heart of Ratanakosin, Wat Arun rising across the river, and Wat Pho offering a calmer encounter with the great reclining Buddha. Then comes the plunge into the city's other rituals, from market browsing and street food to rooftop bars, night bazaars and tuk-tuks. Arriving via Laem Chabang, Bangkok rewards those who embrace its contradictions: chaos and refinement, devotion and nightlife, royal grandeur and everyday appetite.

(O) Wat Arun; (L) At Wat Phra Kaeo, or the temple of the Emerald Buddha; (T) Traders and buyers at Damnoen Saduak Floating Market

Phuket *THAILAND*

(T) Phuket's Big Buddha statue

Phuket is Thailand's blockbuster island, with beaches, diving, dining and nightlife on a scale that can feel almost too polished, with high-rises and consumer buzz sometimes diluting the sense of "Thai-ness". The trick is to use it as both playground and gateway. Offshore, the scattered limestone karsts of Phang Nga Bay form one of the country's top natural wonders, best experienced by sea canoe as you slip into hidden lagoons and shadowy hollows. Back on land, Phuket Town offers a different rhythm, with handsome Sino-Portuguese architecture and a strong Peranakan imprint that hints at the island's tin-mining past and trading routes. Come for the easy island pleasures, stay for the details that give Phuket its deeper character.

Bali (Benoa) *INDONESIA*

Bali has long been the jewel in Indonesia's tourism crown, a small island where elegant temples, verdant landscapes and fine surf underpin the dream. Beyond the beach strips, its cultural centre of gravity is Ubud, where painting, carving, dancing and music-making still form the lifeblood, and the island's classical dance performances are tightly bound to the *gamelan* (a traditional instrument), with every gesture loaded with meaning. Out at sea, Bali also rewards time in the water: it has many good dive sites, and the *Liberty* wreck off Tulamben is the headline act, drawing crowds for its coral-encrusted remains and busy fish life, with shallow sections that suit snorkellers too. Visiting temples demands respect and modest dress, often with sarong and sash. For travellers making a short stop, Bali's appeal is exactly this blend of ritual, art and saltwater spectacle.

(L) Devotions at Tirta Empul Hindu Temple; (T) Taman Ayun Temple; (B) At Sekumpul waterfall

Komodo National Park

INDONESIA

Komodo National Park is one of those places that genuinely feels otherworldly – a scatter of parched, majestic islands off Flores, edged by big skies, dry hills and empty horizons. The headline act is the Komodo dragon, found nowhere else on earth, and seeing one in the wild delivers a proper jolt of Jurassic disbelief. Most visitors land at Loh Liang on Komodo itself, where facilities are geared for the crowds, but longer treks quickly restore the sense of isolation, especially out of high season. The islands' landscapes add to the drama, from tawny ridges and dormant volcanic forms to sheltered bays and the famous pink-sand beaches, where coral fragments blush through the shallows. Underwater, the park is just as charged, with world-class diving and snorkelling in current-swept channels alive with reef fish, turtles, rays and, in the right season, mantas. It is raw, elemental territory, where the scenery feels as primal as the wildlife and the sea is every bit as compelling as the land.

(O) Padar Island; (L) Revelling in the famous pink sands;
(T) A prehistoric-looking Komodo dragon;
(B) Diving over tropical coral reef

Raja Ampat *INDONESIA*

As pristine as they are remote, Raja Ampat feels made for arrival by small ship: a scatter of islands off the western tip of Papua where limestone islets, turquoise lagoons and empty beaches appear in layers from the water. Sorong is the practical gateway, but the real reward lies beyond it, among the karst anchorages of Kabui Bay, the island labyrinth of Misool and the famous viewpoints of Wayag, where the seascape looks almost too intricate to be real. The postcard beauty is only the surface. Beneath it are some of the richest coral reefs on earth, with snorkelling and diving that can bring pygmy seahorses, reef sharks, turtles, mantas and dense clouds of fish in a single day. This is not a place for a casual pier call or a quick city wander; it works best by expedition ship, liveaboard or smaller vessel, with tenders and local boats carrying you into lagoons, villages and reefs. Costs, permits and the long journey to Sorong keep Raja Ampat demanding, but that difficulty is part of the bargain – this is Indonesia at its most marine, remote, and astonishingly alive.

(L) Traditionally dressed Raja Ampat people; (T) Wayag Island's surreal landscape; (B) A shoal of ribbon sweetlips

Tokyo (Yokohama)

JAPAN

Tokyo is a city that barely needs selling, but arriving via Yokohama adds a satisfying shift in perspective, easing you in through Japan's great port-city history before the capital's full-scale intensity takes over. Yokohama is famously cosmopolitan, and its Chinatown – the largest in Japan – is a sensory hit of bright colours, steaming dumplings, temple smoke and street-level bustle, while the waterfront at Minato Mirai gives a cleaner, futuristic counterpoint of towers, promenades and bay views. From there, Tokyo opens up in every direction: Asakusa for Sensō-ji and old-town atmosphere, Ginza for polish, Shibuya for neon and crossing crowds, Harajuku for youth culture, and Ueno for museums and parkland. The wider orbit is just as tempting, with Kamakura's great Buddha and hillside temples, or Nikko's lavish shrines, forests and mountain air. Here, there is deep culture within reach, effortless food at every level, and the chance simply to move through neighbourhoods until the city's momentum takes over.

(O) The crammed, sensory-overload cityscape of Shibuya; (L) A moment of serenity at Asakusa; (T) Tucking in at a vibrant izakaya spot on Omoide Yokocho; (B) The omnipresent form of Mount Fuji

Kyoto & Osaka (Kobe) *JAPAN*

Kyoto is Japan's great cultural anchor: a former imperial capital with an almost overwhelming concentration of temples, gardens, palaces and refined traditions that still shape the city's identity. It can surprise at first, with modern development and industry muddying the classic postcard image, yet the deeper you wander – through old merchant quarters, craft shops, shrine lanes and temple districts – the more Kyoto asserts its quiet authority. Kiyomizu-dera, Fushimi Inari, Arashiyama and the lanes of Higashiyama give the city its enduring drama, especially when cherry blossom beautifies familiar streets. Osaka, close by, supplies the appetite and voltage. It is brasher, funnier and more openly urban, a city of neon canals, railway hubs, basement food halls and late-night eating, where Dotonbori, Kuromon Market and the castle district offer a sharper counterweight to Kyoto's restraint.

(O) Fushimi Inari Shrine in Kyoto; (L) Sightseeing boat in Dotonbori, Osaka; (T) Cherry blossom lines the Philosopher's Path in Kyoto's Higashiyama

Australia, New Zealand & South Pacific

Across Australia, New Zealand and the South Pacific, the sea brings constant shifts in scale and mood: glittering harbours, surf cities, rainforest coasts, reef-bright shallows, glacier-cut fjords and islands that seem to float in blue. Urban energy gives way quickly to wilderness, from eucalyptus hills and coral gardens to Māori landscapes and Polynesian lagoons. The region feels expansive, elemental and sunlit, with beauty often arriving at full volume.

Sydney *AUSTRALIA*

(T) The classic sweep of Sydney Harbour

Sydney isn't shy: a sparkling harbour city with hedonism in its bloodstream, physical beauty on tap, and a sense of self that can feel almost theatrical. The classics deliver every time – the Opera House sails, the Harbour Bridge's steel swagger – but the real addiction is the water itself, best taken in on a ferry to Manly or Watsons Bay as the skyline shifts and the sandstone headlands open around you. Beyond the postcard, Sydney has depth and grit: old stone backstreets in The Rocks, First Nations stories at Barangaroo, Victorian arcades, immigrant food cultures and neighbourhoods that change mood from Surry Hills to Newtown. Its beach life is both lifestyle and spectacle, from Bondi's social theatre to the clifftop walk towards Bronte and Coogee. Even the city's history feels close to the surface, from its long First Nations presence to its convict-era beginnings. Few cities make arrival feel so cinematic.

北京同仁堂
FOR SALE
出售

Melbourne *AUSTRALIA*

Melbourne is Sydney's cooler sibling (literally) – arty, intellectual and quietly magnetic, a city that wins you over through atmosphere rather than big-ticket sights. Its European feel shows in the gardens and boulevards near the centre, while the CBD's modern edges melt into laneways, cafés and neighbourhoods with distinct personalities. Postwar immigration reshaped Melbourne into a true foodie city, and one of its great pleasures is eating your way through Greek, Vietnamese, Lebanese, Italian and more, often in suburbs where the cultural layers are authentic rather than curated. Sport is near-religion here, but so is culture, from festivals to galleries to a year-round calendar that keeps the city humming. In Melbourne, the pleasure is cumulative. Laneway by laneway, coffee by coffee, gallery by gallery, the city reveals itself as somewhere to inhabit rather than simply inspect.

(L) The Heaven archway in Melbourne's Chinatown; (T) Rowing on the Yarra; (B) Flinders Street

Tasmania (Hobart)

AUSTRALIA

Hobart feels like the edge of something: a small, harbour-focused capital with historic warehouses, cold-water light, and Mount Wellington rising behind it like a weather gauge for the whole city. Tasmania's isolation, once seen as a drawback, now reads as an asset, drawing visitors for pristine environments, standout produce, and a creative streak that's helped Hobart develop a quietly confident cultural life. MONA has turbocharged the city's reputation, but the charm is broader than any single attraction, from Salamanca's markets and old port architecture to the simple pleasure of crossing the Derwent towards Bellerive, where beach, marina and cricket ground give the city a sunnier, suburban counterpoint. Beyond town, Tasmania's wider allure is close at hand: wilderness, beaches and the kind of clean-air exhilaration that makes you breathe deeper without thinking. Hobart offers something of a reset – a place that is compact, mountain-backed and entirely free of big-city strain.

(O) View towards Hobart and Mount Wellington. (L) A golden sky above a walkway on Mount Wellington; (T) Stairs into tropical canopy, Mount Wellington; (B) Beach huts in Hobart

Great Barrier Reef (Cairns)

AUSTRALIA

Cairns exists for one reason, and it's a world-class one: access to the Great Barrier Reef, still astonishing in scale and colour despite its fragility. The city itself has a lively, backpacker-dominated buzz, but the real action starts offshore, where day boats and liveaboards fan out to reefs that reward divers and snorkellers alike. You can keep it simple with a cruise excursion and still come away with that first-look reef amazement, coral gardens close enough for snorkelling and deeper sites for those who want tanks and time. What makes Cairns extra-special is the wider setting – the tropical coast where rainforest edges the sea and the sense of nature presses in from every side. It's one of the planet's great sail-and-swim stops, which still offers serious wow factor.

(L) Cairns harbour, a natural jumping off point for the Great Barrier Reef

Whitsundays (Airlie Beach) *AUSTRALIA*

The Whitsundays feel purpose-built for the water. Rainforested island peaks rise from bright blue sea, beaches unfurl in improbable white arcs, and sailing conditions that can turn even a short day trip into a proper escape. Set inside the Great Barrier Reef, the islands offer a rare blend of shelter and spectacle – calm anchorages, vivid shallows, coral gardens and open horizons that encourage you to stop doing and simply look. Airlie Beach is the usual springboard, with Hamilton Island adding a polished resort version, but the real attraction lies on the Whitsundays themselves. Whitehaven Beach is the showpiece, especially from Hill Inlet, where sand and tide swirl into pale, shifting patterns. Elsewhere, catamarans slip between islands, snorkellers drift over fringing reef, and cruisers can watch the light shift from deck. This is Australia at its most postcard-perfect, yet still wildly coastal, ruled by wind, tide, reef and horizon.

(O) Airlie Beach from above; (L) Diving over the Whitsundays' reef; (T) Pristine white sands on the Whitsundays

Milford Sound *NEW ZEALAND*

(T) The mysterious landscape of Milford Sound, with Mitre Peak (or Rahotu) rising above it

Milford Sound, or Piopiotahi, is one of the few places that exceeds its own legend: a slender, glacially carved fiord where vertical walls rise to more than 1,200 metres and waterfalls drop from hanging valleys in silver ropes. It is notoriously wet, but the rain is part of the enchantment. After a downpour, every cliff face seems to sprout water, mist drifts between the peaks, and the whole place becomes less landscape and more theatre. The scale is difficult to absorb from land. You need to be on the water, passing beneath Mitre Peak (Rahotu) and nosing close to Bowen Falls and Stirling Falls, where the spray makes the cliffs feel alive. Despite the crowds, Milford remains mesmerizing, especially if you arrive by the spectacular road from Te Anau and give the fiord time to work on you. It is not merely a bucket-list view, but a place of weather, story, water and scale.

Auckland & Bay of Islands

NEW ZEALAND

Auckland is where most journeys in New Zealand begin. Planes bank over the island-studded Hauraki Gulf and yachts with bright spinnakers tack across the glinting Waitematā Harbour, justifying the "City of Sails" tag. Downtown's high-rises sit among the grassy humps of dozens of extinct volcanoes, with a modest, small-town ease that belies the fact that it is the country's biggest city. South of Auckland, Rotorua adds a very different New Zealand: steaming geothermal valleys, bubbling mud pools, hot springs and one of the country's most important centres of Māori culture. Head north and the mood turns subtropical in the Bay of Islands, 240km away, a scatter of islands in clear blue water that's made for being out on a boat. From Paihia or Russell, small boats head out among six large islands and roughly 140 smaller ones, passing the Black Rocks and the Hole in the Rock, with beaches, dolphins and sheltered blue water giving the bay enduring appeal.

(O) The Sky Tower and Auckland's skyline; (L) A Maori carving; (T) A traditional Maori haka in Rotorua; (B) Bay of Islands

Tahiti & Bora Bora

FRENCH POLYNESIA

These islands are the South Pacific's dream pairing: Tahiti a lush, mountainous gateway and Bora Bora the jewel-box lagoon you've seen on a thousand screen-savers, only brighter in real life. Cruise arrivals (small ships only) heighten the drama, swapping open ocean for reef-protected water that shifts from deep cobalt to electric turquoise as you near shore. Bora Bora's appeal is pure geometry, with a ring of coral reef and *motus* (islets) encircling a lagoon, backed by a volcanic spine that catches the light at sunrise and turns brooding at dusk. The essential pleasures are simple but hard to improve on. Take a lagoon boat trip, spy rays in the shallows and coral gardens below, and admire Mount Otemanu. Tahiti adds depth beyond the beach fantasy, with bigger-island energy, waterfalls, black-sand beaches, viewpoints and markets, plus a cultural confidence that reminds you this isn't just a backdrop.

(O) Over-water accommodation in Bora Bora; (L) A south seas idyll; (T) Shades of blue near Tahiti

Africa & Middle East

Around Africa and the Middle East, the sea frames landscapes of great contrast, taking in mountain-backed cities, desert horizons, souk-scented harbours, coral coasts and islands shaped by spice, trade and empire. Here, Atlantic swell meets dune country, Gulf futurism gives way to Omani restraint, and ancient routes lead inland towards canyons, forts and rose-red stone. Warm, dramatic and richly textured, each arrival carries a sense of adventure.

Cape Town *SOUTH AFRICA*

(T) Bright colours in the Bo-Kaap area of Cape Town

Cape Town comes at you in layers. This lively port city is framed by the blunt bulk of Table Mountain, which the Khoikhoi called Hoerikwaggo, "the mountain in the sea". Up top, the views are spectacular, with docks and the City Bowl laid out beneath, Robben Island offshore and the Atlantic seaboard curling away towards some of Africa's priciest real estate. The city's impact lies in how abruptly it flips from urban to wild: penguins on False Bay, wind-scoured headlands at Cape Point, surf beaches below the Twelve Apostles, and Kirstenbosch spread across the mountain's greener slopes. The Cape Winelands add another register altogether, with Stellenbosch and Franschhoek bringing gabled estates, mountain backdrops and long lunches within easy reach. Back in town, the Bo-Kaap's minarets and colour-washed terraces add history and texture, while the V&A Waterfront and Long Street keep the "Mother City" buzzing all day and evening.

Walvis Bay *NAMIBIA*

Walvis Bay looks workaday at first glance – Namibia's main port is all businesslike streets and fishing-industry grit. Then you reach the lagoon, one of southern Africa's precious coastal wetlands, and the place changes gear. In summer, the shallows and salt pans can hold well over a hundred thousand birds, with flamingos stealing the show amid pelicans, terns and waders. Out on the water, kayaking and cruises slip you past dolphins and Cape fur seals at Pelican Point, the sandspit that shelters the lagoon from the Atlantic beyond. The ultimate day out heads south by 4x4 to Sandwich Harbour, where towering dunes pitch straight into the surf in a landscape that feels half desert, half ocean.

(L, T) Flamingos and fur seals in Walvis Bay's lagoon; (B) SUVs are needed for traversing Nambia's sands

Dubai *UAE*

Dubai is the rare cruise port that feels like a city still being invented. In barely half a century it has jumped from small Gulf trading centre to a glossy, record-breaking metropolis, powered by petro-dollars, commercial swagger and unembarrassed ambition. The headlines are familiar: Burj Khalifa skewering the sky, the Burj al Arab's sail-shaped silhouette, the Palm Jumeirah drawn like a logo offshore. What makes a day ashore memorable is the contrast. Along the Creek, Old Dubai still deals in textures and smells, from wind-towered heritage houses to the Gold and Spice souks, and the simple pleasure of skimming across the water on an *abra* while cargo-laden *dhows* crowd the banks. Then, minutes later, the hyper-futurism of Sheikh Zayed Road turns the city into something that resembles science fiction.

(L) The sail-shape of the famous Burj al Arab in Jumeirah; (T) Downtown Dubai's skyline; (B) A traditional abra on the creek

Muscat

OMAN

Muscat doesn't announce itself with a skyline so much as a long coastal unfurling, with low-rise white neighbourhoods strung between the sea and red-rock hills that can look almost lunar in the heat. Its appeal lies where Oman's maritime past and modern confidence overlap. Muttrah is the natural starting point, with its sweeping corniche, *dhows* in the harbour and the plunge into Muttrah Souk, a maze of frankincense, perfumes, silver *khanjars*, lanterns and folded cloth. Further along the coast, Old Muscat feels deliberately set apart, tucked behind craggy mountains and watched over by the twin Portuguese forts of Al Jalali and Al Mirani. Here, restored walls, a calm government quarter and ceremonial Al Alam Palace give the city a stately hush. The Sultan Qaboos Grand Mosque adds a grander register, with marble courtyards, intricate tilework and a prayer hall of immense quiet.

(O) Sultan Qaboos Grand Mosque in Muscat; (L) Mosaic Omani lanterns in the souk; (T) Traditional dhows by the Muttrah corniche

Aqaba

JORDAN

Aqaba is Jordan's slim Red Sea window, a beach-town counterpoint to the inland drama of desert and rock. For most visitors, the water is the reason to pause here. Along the short coastline south of town, reefs shelve gently from the beach, making snorkelling easy and diving welcoming even for first-timers. The corals remain in notably good condition below the six-metre line, with biodiversity to match, and almost nine kilometres of the south coast sits within the protected Aqaba Marine Park. On land, the sights are modest but engaging. The Corniche and the public beach north of the flagpole square give a sense of local life, especially on Fridays, with families strolling, radios playing and children selling snacks. Aqaba also works beautifully as a gateway to the region, taking in warm Red Sea shallows one day, then Petra's carved façades or Wadi Rum's vast red-sand silence the next.

(O, L) Aqaba's port; (T) Camels at dusk in Wadi Rum; (B) Decorative boats tied up on the bay

Zanzibar (Stone Town)

TANZANIA

Stone Town is one of those places where getting lost is really the point. The old quarter, Mji Mkongwe, is an Arabian-style labyrinth of twisting lanes, bazaars and grand mansions, much of it built on nineteenth-century wealth and the brutal commerce of slavery. Along the waterfront, the town turns ceremonial, with palaces facing the sea and a brooding Omani fort holding the line, a façade the sultans intended visitors to admire. Step a hundred metres inland and the mood shifts again: decaying houses, carved doors, small shops, damp-stained walls and sudden courtyards that feel half hidden. There's history you can't dodge, from the site of Africa's last slave market to churches tied to abolition, yet the town is also sprightly, lived-in and endlessly photogenic. Add easy access to reefs and spice-scented island life, and Stone Town becomes more than a historic showpiece: it is Zanzibar's memory, marketplace and threshold to the Indian Ocean.

(L) Rooftops in Stone Town

Port Louis *MAURITIUS*

Port Louis isn't a prettified capital, and that's part of its pull. It is still a working port, with freighters in the basin and a dense city packed between sea and the Moka Mountains, crowded, noisy and full of daily hustle. Not long ago it was notorious for shutting down early, but a local lift has given it a more polished focal point in the Caudan Waterfront, where cafés, shops, museums and evening lights soften the edges. The real character, though, lies beyond the waterfront gloss: a jumble of new towers and creaking old buildings, mosques, churches and temples, Chinese and Muslim quarters, and, above all, the lively central market. Within easy reach, the Sir Seewoosagur Ramgoolam Botanical Garden in Pamplemousses offers giant water lilies and colonial-era calm, while the Eureka House gives a gentler glimpse of plantation history in the green foothills. Give Port Louis half a day and an excursion beyond the city, and you'll leave with a sharper sense of Mauritius than any resort beach can offer.

(L) Kaylasson temple, Port Louis; (T) Blue Bay, a resort area near the capital; (B) Mauritius's mountainous interior

Publishing information

The World by Sea •
100 Legendary Cruise Destinations
Editor: Sarah Clark
Proofreader: Rachel Lawrence
Designer: Michał Ptasznik
Picture Editor: Piotr Kala
Picture Manager: Tom Smyth
Production Operations Manager: Katie Bennett
Publishing Technology Manager: Rebeka Davies
Head of Publishing: Sarah Clark

Our selection
The World by Sea • 100 Legendary Cruise Destinations offers our edit of the most exceptional ports of call around the world, with choices and content curated from our extensive Rough Guides list.

First Edition 2026

ISBN: 9781835296493

Printed by Finidr in Czech Republic

A catalogue record for this book is available from the British Library.

MIX
Paper | Supporting responsible forestry
FSC® C014138
FSC www.fsc.org

DISTRIBUTION
UK, Ireland and Europe
Apa Publications (UK) Ltd; mail@roughguides.com
United States and Canada
Two Rivers; ips@ ingramcontent.com
Australia and New Zealand
Woodslane; info@woodslane.com.au
Worldwide
Apa Publications (UK) Ltd; mail@roughguides.com

SPECIAL SALES, CONTENT LICENSING AND COPUBLISHING
Rough Guides can be purchased in bulk quantities at discounted prices. We can create special editions, personalized jackets and corporate imprints tailored to your needs.
mail@roughguides.com; http://roughguides.com

EU REPRESENTATIVE
LOGOS EUROPE, 9 rue Nicolas Poussin, 17000, LA ROCHELLE, France
Contact@logoseurope.eu; +33 (0) 667937378

Photo credits

All images Shutterstock except:
Alamy 10/11
Kenny Lam/Visit Scotland 62, 67BL

Cover credit: Cruise ship in Sunnylvsfjorden, gateway to Geirangerfjord, Norway **iStock**

Caption key
(L) = left
(R) = right
(T) = top
(B) = bottom
(O) = opposite

THE **World**
IS **waiting**

Make the **legend**
your own